Kaplan Publishing are constantly finding new ways to make a difference to your studies and our exciting online resources really do offer something different to students looking for exam success.

This book comes with free MyKaplan online resources so that you can study anytime, anywhere. **This free online resource is not sold separately and is included in the price of the book.**

Having purchased this book, you have access to the following online study materials:

CONTENT	ACCA (including FBT, FMA, FFA)		FIA (excluding FBT, FMA, FFA)	
	Text	Kit	Text	Kit
Electronic version of the book	✓	✓	✓	✓
Knowledge checks with instant answers	✓		✓	
Material updates	✓	✓	✓	✓
Latest official ACCA exam questions*		✓		
Pocket Notes (digital copy)	✓		✓	
Study Planner	✓			
Progress Test including questions and answers	✓		✓	
Syllabus recap Videos		✓		✓
Revision Planner		✓		✓
Question Debrief and Walkthrough Videos		✓		
Mock Exam including questions and answers		✓		

* Excludes BT, MA, FA, FBT, FMA, FFA; for all other papers includes a selection of questions, as released by ACCA

How to access your online resources

Received this book as part of your Kaplan course?
If you have a MyKaplan account, your full online resources will be added automatically, in line with the information in your course confirmation email. If you've not used MyKaplan before, you'll be sent an activation email once your resources are ready.

Bought your book from Kaplan?
We'll automatically add your online resources to your MyKaplan account. If you've not used MyKaplan before, you'll be sent an activation email.

Bought your book from elsewhere?
Go to **www.mykaplan.co.uk/add-online-resources**
Enter the ISBN number found on the title page and back cover of this book.
Add the unique pass key number contained in the scratch panel below.
You may be required to enter additional information during this process to set up or confirm your account details.

This code can only be used once for the registration of this book online. This registration and your online content will expire when the examinations covered by this book have taken place. Please allow one hour from the time you submit your book details for us to process your request.

Please scratch the film to access your unique code.

Please be aware that this code is case-sensitive and you will need to include the dashes within the passcode, but not when entering the ISBN.

AF871986

KAPLAN PUBLISHING

ACCA Diploma in Financial and Management Accounting (RQF Level 3)

FA2

Maintaining Financial Records

EXAM KIT

KAPLAN PUBLISHING

British Library Cataloguing-in-Publication Data

A catalogue record for this book is available from the British Library.

Published by:
Kaplan Publishing UK
179–191 Borough High Street,
London,
SE1 1HR

ISBN: 978-1-83735-263-0

Acknowledgements

We are grateful to the Association of Chartered Certified Accountants and the Chartered Institute of Management Accountants for permission to reproduce past examination questions. The answers have been prepared by Kaplan Publishing.

INTRODUCTION

Packed with questions, this book will help you to successfully prepare for your examination.

- All questions are grouped by syllabus topics.
- Objective test questions are of exam standard and format – this enables you to master the examination techniques.

The exam kit begins with some short revision questions to ensure you will get the most from the exam standard questions when you attempt them. Start by attempting the revision questions. Marks are given as an indication of the difficulty of the question.

When you have completed section 1, revision questions, and you have revised any areas of difficulty as highlighted by this exercise, you may attempt section 2 comprising objective test questions.

Note that for 2026-27, where the detail of the syllabus for this exam has been updated, this exam kit reflects the changes to the syllabus.

For further information about the FA2 examination please refer to ACCA website:

www.accaglobal.com

ENHANCEMENTS

We have added the following enhancement to the answers in this exam kit:

Tutorial note

Some answers include tutorial notes to explain some of the technical points in more detail.

CONTENTS

Section

This document references IFRS® Accounting Standards and IAS® Accounting Standards which are authored by the International Accounting Standards Board (the board) and issued prior to 31 August 2025.

Quality and accuracy are of the utmost importance to us so if you spot an error in any of our products, please send an email to mykaplanreporting@kaplan.com with full details.

Our Quality Co-ordinator will work with our technical team to verify the error and take action to ensure it is corrected in future editions.

INDEX TO QUESTIONS AND ANSWERS

SYLLABUS AND REVISION GUIDANCE

SYLLABUS CONTENT

FA2 *Maintaining Financial Records* introduces the fundamental principles of accounting and develops the knowledge and understanding required to maintain accounting records. You will learn to produce accounting records, extract a trial balance and make necessary adjustments to produce an extended trial balance and basic financial statements. The syllabus covers accounting for the business transactions of sole traders and partnerships.

A ACCOUNTING PRINCIPLES, CONCEPTS AND CHARACTERISTICS

1 The key accounting principles and characteristics

(a) Explain the accounting principles of accounting.

- (i) Going concern
- (ii) Accruals
- (iii) Materiality
- (iv) Consistency
- (v) Prudence
- (vi) Duality
- (vii) Business entity
- (vii) Historical cost

(b) Explain the qualitative accounting characteristics relating to.

- (i) Relevance
- (ii) Faithful representation
- (iii) Comparability
- (iv) Verifiability
- (v) Timeliness
- (vi) Understandability

2 Maintaining financial records

(a) Explain the importance of maintaining financial records for internal and external use.

(b) Describe the type of accounting records that a business should maintain and the main uses of the records.

(c) Describe the key features of a computerised accounting system, including the use of external servers to store data (the cloud).

3 The regulatory framework

(a) Describe the main requirements of IFRS® Accounting Standards in relation to syllabus area D.

B THE PRINCIPLES AND PROCESS OF DOUBLE-ENTRY BOOKKEEPING

1 The elements of the financial statements

(a) Explain the meaning of the accounting equation and demonstrate its impact on double-entry bookkeeping.

(b) Describe the meaning of income, expenses, assets, liabilities and capital in an accounting context.

(c) Describe the components of a set of final accounts for a sole trader.

2 Recording financial data and the flow of accounting information in the production of financial statements

(a) Explain how financial data is initially recorded in the accounting system.

(b) Identify reasons for closing off accounts and producing a trial balance.

(c) Explain the process of preparing a set of final statements from a trial balance.

C THE PREPARATION OF JOURNAL ENTRIES AND GENERAL LEDGER ACCOUNTS

1 Preparation of journals entries

(a) Prepare journals to record transactions in an appropriate format.

2 Preparation of general ledger accounts

(a) Explain the purpose and use of general ledger accounts.

(b) Post journals entries into the appropriate general ledger account.

(c) Illustrate the year end procedures on the general ledger accounts bringing forward and carrying forward balances as appropriate.

D RECORDING TRANSACTIONS AND EVENTS

1 Sales and purchases

(a) Record sale and purchases transactions.

(b) Record sales and purchase returns.

(c) Account for discounts received.

(d) Account for the following discounts allowed to customers in accordance with IFRS® Accounting Standards (i) trade discounts (ii) settlement discounts.

(e) Identify sources of information on sales tax and explain the relationship between the entity and the relevant government agency (revenue/tax authority).

(f) Explain the general principles of the operation of a sales tax, including:

- (i) requirements for registration
- (ii) main information to be included on business documentation
- (iii) types of taxable supplies and their classification for sales tax
- (iv) accounting and payment of sales tax
- (v) penalties for late returns or late payment sales tax.

(g) Explain the different methods of accounting and reporting for sales tax.

(h) Identify and obtain sales tax data from the accounting system.

(i) Calculate sales tax on inputs (purchases) and output (sales, enter the appropriate information into the accounting system and calculate the sales tax to/from the business.

(j) Illustrate the main components of a sales tax return.

(k) Calculate the cash flow impact on the business of the payment of sales tax and the potential impact on the business of any changes in legislation for sales tax.

2 Cash and bank

(a) Record cash and bank transactions in general ledger accounts.

(b) Report cash and bank balances in the financial statements.

3 Inventories

(a) Describe the need for adjustments for inventory in preparing financial statements.

(b) Record cost of sales and closing inventories.

(c) Identify and apply the alternative methods of valuing inventories.

(d) Explain and apply the requirements of IFRS® Accounting Standards for valuing inventories.

(e) Identify which costs should be included when measuring inventories.

(f) Explain the use of continuous and period end inventory records.

(g) Calculate the value of closing inventories using FIFO (first in, first out) and AVCO (average cost) both periodic weighted average and continuous weighted average.

(h) Identify the impact of inventory valuation methods on profit, assets and capital including:

   (i) periodic weighted average

   (ii) continuous weighted average

   (iii) FIFO.

(i) Report inventories in the final accounts.

4 Tangible non-current assets and depreciation

(a) Define non-current assets.

(b) Explain the difference between current and non-current assets.

(c) Explain the difference between asset expenditure (capitalised) and expense items.

(d) Classify expenditure as asset expenditure (capitalised) or expenses charged to profit or loss.

(e) Explain the impact of misclassification of asset expenditure as expenses and vice versa on the statement of profit or loss and the statement of financial position.

(f) Prepare journal entries to record the acquisition and disposal of non-current assets (including part exchange) in accordance with IFRS® Accounting Standards.

(g) Calculate and record gains or losses on disposal of non-current assets in the statement of profit or loss including part exchange transactions and scrapping of assets.

(h) Explain the purpose of depreciation.

(i) Calculate the charge for depreciation using straight line and reducing balance methods.

(j) Identify the circumstances where different methods of calculating depreciation would be appropriate.

(k) Illustrate how the depreciation charge and accumulated depreciation are recorded in general ledger accounts.

(l) Explain the purpose and function of an asset register.

(m) Prepare the non-current asset register accounting for all or part of the following:

  (i) acquisition including authorisation

  (ii) part exchange and cash non-current asset purchases

  (iii) depreciation.

(n) Identify and resolve any discrepancies relating to the accounting records for non-current assets.

(o) Report non-current assets and depreciation in the financial statements.

5 Accrued expenses, prepaid expenses, accrued income and deferred income

(a) Apply the accrual accounting to accruals, prepayments, accrued income and deferred income.

(b) Calculate the adjustments needed for accruals, prepayments, accrued income and deferred income when preparing financial statements.

(c) Illustrate the Illustrate the process of adjusting for accruals, prepayments, accrued income and deferred income when preparing financial statements.

(d) Prepare the manual journal entries and update the general ledger accounts for the creation and reversal of accruals, prepayments, accrued income and deferred income.

(e) Identify the impact of accruals, prepayments, accrued income and deferred income on profit and net assets.

(f) Report accruals, prepayments, accrued income and deferred income in the financial statements.

6 Receivables, payables and provisions

(a) Explain and identify examples of receivables and payables.

(b) Prepare manual journal entries to write off an irrecoverable debt.

(c) Prepare the manual journal entry to record an irrecoverable debt later recovered.

(d) Identify the impact of irrecoverable debts on the statement of profit or loss and on the statement of financial position.

(e) Calculate the movement in the allowance for receivables and the closing balance.

(f) Prepare manual journal entries to create and adjust an allowance for receivables.

(g) Illustrate how to include movements in the allowance for receivables in the statement of profit or loss and how the closing balance of the allowance should be reported in the statement of financial position.

(h) Account for contras between trade receivables and trade payables.

(i) Explain the nature of provisions and liabilities in accordance with IFRS® Accounting Standards.

(j) Distinguish between a provision and other liabilities.

(k) Account for provisions and other liabilities.

(i) Report provisions and other liabilities in the financial statements.

7 Capital and finance costs

(a) Distinguish between capital injected by the business owner(s) and amounts received from third parties for an unincorporated business (sole trader/partnership).

(b) Demonstrate the impact of changes in capital on the financial statements.

(c) Prepare the capital general ledger account for an unincorporated business.

E RECONCILIATIONS

1 Bank reconciliations

(a) Explain the purpose of reconciling the bank general ledger account to the corresponding bank statement or internet banking records.

(b) Prepare the reconciliation of the bank general ledger account to the bank statement or internet banking records.

(c) Identify errors and omissions in the bank general ledger account and the bank statement or internet banking records.

(d) Identify timing differences in a bank reconciliation.

(e) Make correcting entries in the bank general ledger account.

(f) Identify the bank balance to be reported in the financial statements.

2 Trade payables account reconciliations

(a) Explain the purpose of reconciling the balances on individual supplier accounts to external documents.

(b) Prepare a reconciliation of the balances on individual supplier accounts to supplier statements.

(c) Identify errors and omissions in the trade payables general ledger account and supplier statements.

(d) Make correcting entries in the trade payables general ledger account.

(e) Identify the trade payables balance to be reported in the financial statements.

F PREPARING A TRIAL BALANCE AND CORRECTING ERRORS

1 Preparing a trial balance

(a) Explain the purpose of the trial balance.

(b) Distinguish between errors which will be detected by extracting a trial balance and those which will not.

(c) Calculate and explain the impact of errors on the statement of profit or loss and the statement of financial position.

(d) Identify the limitations of the trial balance.

(e) Prepare the initial trial balance.

(f) Explain the process of finalising the trial balance.

(g) Explain and record year-end adjustments on the trial balance, including: (i) Inventories, (ii) Non-current asset transactions, (iii) Depreciation, (iv) Accruals, prepayments, accrued income and deferred income (v) Allowance for receivables, (vi) Irrecoverable debts (vii) Provisions.

(h) Prepare a final trial balance including calculating the final reported profit or loss.

(i) Prepare the opening trial balance for the next accounting period.

2 Correction of errors using manual journal entries

(a) Explain the purpose of, and reasons for, creating a suspense account.

(b) Identify different types of bookkeeping error including those that result in suspense accounts.

(c) Describe the action required to correct errors including clearing any suspense accounts.

(d) Prepare correcting manual journal entries and update the general ledger accounts and trial balance for any corrections made entries.

(e) Explain how the financial statements are affected by the correction of errors.

G PREPARING FINANCIAL STATEMENTS

1 Preparation of the financial statements including incomplete records

(a) Explain the process of preparing a set of financial statements from a trial balance.

(b) Explain the format and purpose of the statement of profit or loss and the statement of financial position for a sole trader.

(c) Prepare the financial statements for a sole trader from a trial balance.

(d) Describe the circumstances which lead to incomplete records.

(e) Describe the methods of constructing accounts from incomplete records.

(f) Prepare the Prepare the financial statements or elements thereof using incomplete record techniques such as:(i) Mark ups and margins, (ii) General ledger accounts to derive missing figures, (iii) Manipulation of the accounting equation.

H PARTNERSHIPS

1 Partnership agreement

(a) Define a partnership.

(b) Explain the purpose and content of a partnership agreement.

(c) Explain, calculate and account for appropriations of profit: (i) Salaries of partners, (ii) Interest on drawings, (iii) Interest on capital, (iv) Share of residual profit or loss.

2 Partnership accounting records

(a) Explain the difference between partners' capital and current accounts.

(b) Prepare the partners' capital and current accounts.

3 Partnership financial statements and change in partnership

(a) Prepare the financial statements for a partnership.

(b) Explain and account for the admission of a new partner including the treatment of any goodwill arising.

Note: Candidates will not be expected to calculate the value of goodwill in a partnership.

PLANNING YOUR REVISION

Begin by asking yourself two questions:

How much time do I have available for revision?

Remember to take into account:

- times of the day when you work most effectively
- other commitments
- time definitely unavailable (e.g. holidays)
- relaxation time.

What do I need to cover during my revision?

Remember to take into account that:

- all syllabus areas are equally examinable
- you need more time when revising areas of the syllabus you feel least confident about
- question practice is the best form of revision.

Make a timetable/plan to remind yourself how much work you have to do and when you are free to do it. Allow some time for slippage.

REVISION TECHNIQUES

- Go through your notes and textbook highlighting the important points.
- You might want to produce your own set of **summarised notes**.
- **List key words** for each topic to remind you of the essential concepts.
- **Practise exam-standard questions**, under timed conditions.
- **Rework questions** that you got completely wrong the first time, but only when you think you know the subject better.
- If you get stuck on topics, **find someone to explain** them to you (your tutor or a colleague, for example).
- **Read recent articles** on the ACCA website or in the student magazine.
- **Read** good newspapers and professional journals.

THE EXAMINATION

FORMAT OF THE EXAM

The format of the computer-based exam is as follows: Total time allowed: 2 hours.

	Number of marks
50 compulsory objective test questions (2 marks each)	100

Answering the questions

- **Objective test questions** – read the questions carefully and work through any calculations required. If you have a choice of answers and don't know the answer, then guess.
- **Data entry questions –** ensure that you attempt all questions – if necessary try to do the calculations, even if you are unsure.
- **If you get stuck with a question** skip it and return to it later.
- **Answer every question** – if you do not know the answer, you do not lose anything by guessing. Towards the end of the examination spend the last five minutes reading through your answers and making any corrections.
- **Equally divide the time** you spend on questions. In a two-hour examination that has 50 questions you have about 2.4 minutes per a question.
- **Do not skip any part of the syllabus** and make sure that you have **learnt** definitions, **know** key words and their meanings and importance, and **understand** the names and meanings of rules, concepts and theories.
- Bear in mind that this exam includes both narrative and computational questions, so ensure that you are able to deal with both types of question.

Computer-based examinations

- Be sure you understand how to use the **software** before you start the exam. If in doubt, ask the assessment centre staff to explain it to you.
- Questions are **displayed on the screen** and answers are entered using keyboard and mouse. At the end of the exam, you are given a certificate showing the result you have achieved.
- **Don't panic** if you realise you've answered a question incorrectly – you can always go back and change your answer.
- The CBE question types are as follows:
  - Multiple choice – where you are required to choose one answer from a list of options provided by clicking on the appropriate 'radio button'
  - Multiple response – where you are required to select more than one response from the options provided by clicking on the appropriate tick boxes(typically choose two options from the available list
  - Multiple response matching – where you are required to indicate a response to a number of related statements by clicking on the 'radio button' which corresponds to the appropriate response for each statement
  - Number entry – where you are required to key in a response to a question shown on the screen.

ACCA SUPPORT

Note that from 2025-26, the detail of the syllabus for this exam has been updated. This exam kit reflects the changes to the syllabus.

For additional support with your studies please also refer to the ACCA Global website.

Section 1

REVISION QUESTIONS – SECTION A

ACCOUNTING PRINCIPLES AND CONCEPTS

1 State two ways in which IFRS Accounting Standards improve financial accounting. **(3 marks)**

2 Briefly explain the going concern concept. **(2 marks)**

3 The *Conceptual Framework for Financial Reporting* states that in order to be useful, financial information should have the following fundamental and enhancing qualitative characteristics:

(i) relevance

(ii) faithful representation

(iii) comparability

(iv) verifiability

(v) timelines, and

(vi) understandability.

Briefly explain any two of these qualitative characteristics. **(4 marks)**

4 Briefly explain the business entity concept and its impact on the recording of transactions. **(2 marks)**

5 Explain why every transaction is recorded using both a debit entry and a credit entry. **(3 marks)**

BASIC BOOKKEEPING

6 Define the terms 'asset' and 'liability', and provide one example of each. **(4 marks)**

7 Explain how each element of the accounting equation is affected when goods for resale are purchased on credit. **(3 marks)**

8 Explain how settlement discounts should be treated when an entity is raising a sales invoice and the customer is not expected to take advantage of the early settlement discount offered. **(3 marks)**

9 Explain how settlement discounts should be treated when an entity is raising a sales invoice and the customer is expected to take advantage of the early settlement discount offered. **(3 marks)**

NON-CURRENT ASSETS AND DEPRECIATION

10 Give three reasons why there may be a difference between the assets listed on the non-current asset register and the physical presence of assets. **(3 marks)**

11 Your friend, a self-employed garage mechanic, has recently disposed of an old set of car ramps. Your friend is unsure how to calculate whether this resulted in a profit or loss on disposal.

Briefly explain to your friend what factors would need to be accounted for when calculating the profit or loss on disposal. **(4 marks)**

12 Calculate the annual depreciation charge for five years, for a non-current asset costing $15,000, to be depreciated at a rate of 25% using the reducing balance method. **(4 marks)**

RECONCILIATIONS AND ERRORS

13 You are helping a friend, a self-employed hairdresser, with financial record keeping. You notice that your friend posted the purchase of a new set of adjustable chairs for the salon to the repairs account. You bring this error to the attention of your friend.

Briefly explain what type of error this is and why it is important to correct this posting in the accounts. **(3 marks)**

14 A friend of yours in business as an hotelier notes that whenever a bank statement is received, the balance rarely agrees with that shown in the bank general ledger account balance.

Briefly explain the reason for such differences. **(3 marks)**

ADJUSTMENTS TO THE TRIAL BALANCE

15 Explain the main purpose of a trial balance. **(2 marks)**

16 Briefly explain the differences between an irrecoverable debt and an allowance for receivables and the accounting treatment of each. **(4 marks)**

17 The inventory sheet of a business retailing children's clothes showed a batch of summer t-shirts at a cost of $300. It seems clear that these will be later included in a sale and will be expected to realise $180 in total.

Briefly explain at what value the t-shirts should be correctly shown in the inventory valuation and what principle it is based upon. **(2 marks)**

18 A friend of yours recently reviewed a set of final accounts. Your friend does not understand why, on the statement of financial position, there are terms like accruals and prepayments.

Explain which accounting concept has been applied here and the purpose of this principle when drafting first accounts. **(3 marks)**

FINAL ACCOUNTS

19 State the purpose of:

(i) the statement of profit or loss; and

(ii) the statement of financial position. **(2 marks)**

20 A significant difference between the statement of financial position of a sole trader and that of a partnership is that a partnership's statement of financial position includes the partners' current accounts.

Explain what entries are made in a partner's current account and what a closing credit balance would represent. **(2 marks)**

21 What are the principal contents of a partnership agreement? **(2 marks)**

22 State the five steps that should be followed when determining when, and how much, revenue should be recognised in the financial statements. **(3 marks)**

23 Explain the differences between the items accounted for in the capital and current accounts of a partner. **(3 marks)**

Section 2

OBJECTIVE TEST QUESTIONS – SECTION B

ACCOUNTING PRINCIPLES AND CONCEPTS

1 **Which accounting principle is described by the following statement?**

'It is a threshold quality that requires information is disclosed if it is likely to affect decisions made by users of financial statements.'

A Prudence

B Materiality

C Going concern

D Business entity

2 **The principle of consistency is best described by which of the following statements?**

A Transactions should be accounted for on a consistent basis within an accounting period only.

B Transactions should be accounted for on a consistent basis from one accounting period to another.

C Transactions relating to the statement of financial position only should be accounted for on a consistent basis.

D Transactions should be accounted for on a consistent basis, both within an accounting period, and from one accounting period to another.

3 **Which accounting principle is described by the following statement?**

'For accounting purposes, a business is separate from its owners.'

A Going concern

B Materiality

C Business entity

D Prudence

4 The *Conceptual Framework for Financial Reporting* includes guidance on how assets and liabilities should be classified in the financial statements.

How should each of the following items be classified for inclusion in the financial statements?

	Statement of profit or loss	Statement of financial position
Expenses		
Equity		

5 **Which of the following statements best explains the going concern principle?**

A The business is not expected to continue operating for the foreseeable future.

B There is a reasonable expectation that the business will continue operating for the foreseeable future.

C It is guaranteed that the business will continue operating for the foreseeable future.

D The business will terminate its operating activities within the foreseeable future.

6 **Which of the following statements best explains the historical cost principle?**

A It is represented by the cost of an asset when it was purchased

B It is represented by the cost of replacing an asset

C It is represented by the current market value of an asset

D It is represented by net realisable value of an asset

7 A business included within its closing inventory valuation some goods that were received before the year end, but invoices were not received until after the year end, but an accrual was recognised.

Which accounting concept is this in accordance with?

A the historical cost concept

B the accruals concept

C the consistency concept

D the materiality concept

8 **Which of the following statements best explains the importance of maintaining financial records?**

A Financial records should be maintained for the sole purpose of enabling the business owner to make management and control decisions.

B Financial records should be maintained for the sole purpose of enabling the business owner to make information available to external interested parties.

C Financial records should be maintained for the sole purpose of enabling the business owner to determine any tax liability arising.

D Financial records should be maintained to enable a business owner to make decisions regarding the business and to make information available to interested external parties when appropriate to do so.

9 **Which of the following statements is NOT true in relation to the importance of a proprietor maintaining financial records for internal use?**

A Accounting records enable the proprietor to manage and control the business

B Accounting records enable the proprietor to reconcile the bank and cash balances

C Accounting records enable the proprietor to make investment decisions regarding the business

D Accounting records enable the proprietor to provide information that may be of interest to the general public

10 **Which of the following statements is NOT true in relation to the importance of a proprietor maintaining financial records for external use?**

A They enable the proprietor to provide information to lenders and creditors of the business to support credit and loan applications.

B They enable the proprietor to make investment decisions relating to the business.

C They enable the proprietor to provide information to the tax authorities relevant to the business.

D They enable interested parties, such as the general public, to review and evaluate the financial and economic impact that the business has upon the community.

11 **What is the purpose of a credit note?**

A It acknowledges a purchase on credit

B It is a reference from an agency detailing the creditworthiness of a new customer

C It is issued when a deposit is paid on goods

D It is issued to cancel all or part of a sales invoice

12 Which TWO items below identify the purpose of a purchase invoice?

	Selected answer
To reclaim the sales tax	
To record how much is owed by the customer	
To identify the goods bought	
To record how much is owed from the customer	

13 Kaz received a document from Cullen's Stationery Supplies for eight reams of paper which had been supplied three previously. How should Kaz refer to this document?

A It is a goods received note

B It is a receipt

C It is a purchase invoice

D It is a credit note

14 Why must a business retain documents?

A To enable customer and supplier queries to be answered

B For historical purposes

C It is a requirement of accounting and tax law

D To facilitate planning

15 Which of the following are fundamental qualitative characteristics of financial information according to the *Conceptual Framework for Financial Reporting*?

(i) Relevance

(ii) Reliability

A (i) and (ii)

B (i) only

C Neither (i) nor (ii)

D (ii) only

16 How should each of the following items be classified according to the *Conceptual Framework for Financial Reporting*?

	Fundamental qualitative characteristic	Enhancing qualitative characteristic
Understandability		
Faithful representation		

17 Which TWO of the following are enhancing qualitative characteristics of financial information according to the *Conceptual Framework for Financial Reporting*?

	Selected answer
Going concern	
Comparability	
Timeliness	
Relevance	

18 Which TWO of the following are enhancing qualitative characteristics of financial information according to the *Conceptual Framework for Financial Reporting*?

	Selected answer
Verifiability	
Materiality	
Historical cost	
Understandability	

19 Which TWO of the following are fundamental qualitative characteristics of financial information according to the *Conceptual Framework for Financial Reporting*?

	Selected answer
Relevance	
Reliability	
Faithful representation	
Verifiability	

20 Which one of the following is an advantage of cloud accounting?

A Employees of the cloud service provider can access the data of any entity it supports

B The sharing of data and files can be done easily by multiple users

C There is no risk of the cloud service provider suffering a cyber attack

D There is no risk of the cloud service provider suffering a breach of security

21 Which one of the following is a definition of cloud accounting?

A Cloud accounting is all computerised accounting systems and processes

B cloud accounting is accounting hardware and software supplied by an external third party

C Cloud accounting is accounting software that is provided by an external third party

D Cloud accounting is access to accounting systems and processes and data storage on remote servers

22 Which one of the following is a disadvantage of cloud accounting?

A A cloud service provider will provide services to more than one client

B It is not possible for multiple user in multiple locations to access the services

C All clients of the cloud service provider are reliant upon the financial stability of the service provider to continue to provide services

D The cloud service provider does not need to comply with data protection regulations

23 A computerised accounting system produces a statement of account for each credit customer, which is then issued to each customer as a reminder to pay amounts due.

Which one of the following is an advantage of this system?

A The statements are produced independently from the sales system

B All amounts due will be received from customers

C Each statement is based upon data recorded in the general ledger

D None of the statements will contain errors or omissions

24 The employees of Manx Co use a personal smart fob to record the time they arrive and leave work each day. This information is then used by the automated wages system to produce the monthly payroll totals and payslips.

Which one of the following is an advantage of this system?

A The processing of payroll information and payslips is more efficient and reliable than a manual system

B An employee will never forget to use their personal smart fob

C Supervisors no longer need to review and approve working hours for each employee

D It is not possible for there to be any errors in the payroll totals and payslips produced

25 Coypu Co is an online video games retailer and operates a computerised accounting system, which includes integrated sales and inventory systems. It maintains an inventory of over 5,000 items, across an extensive range of video games.

Which one of the following is not an advantage of a computerised accounting system?

A Sales to individual customers are straightforward to record

B It is easy to trace and track orders for new games from individual customers

C The inventory system can be interrogated quickly and easily to confirm the inventory level of any game at any time

D Computerised accounting records are never wrong

PRINCIPLES AND PROCESSES OF BASIC BOOKKEEPING

26 Which of the following statements best describes current assets?

A Assets which are currently located on the business premises

B Assets which are used to conduct the organisation's current business

C Assets which are expected to be converted into cash in the short term

D Assets which are not expected to be converted into cash in the short term

27 Which of the following statements best describes non-current assets?

A Assets which are used in the business over a number of accounting periods to undertake the activities of the organisation.

B Assets which are used to conduct the organisation's current business.

C Assets which are expected to be converted into cash in the short term.

D Assets which can be used to convert into cash in the short-term or to be used in the business over a number of accounting periods.

28 Which of the following statements best describes non-current liabilities?

A Liabilities which have not yet been incurred, but which will be incurred with the next twelve months.

B Liabilities which will only be paid upon termination of a business.

C Liabilities which will fall due for payment within twelve months of the reporting date.

D Liabilities which will fall due for payment after more than twelve months from the reporting date.

29 Which of the following statements best describes a current liability?

A It is a liability which has not yet been incurred, but which will be incurred with the next twelve months.

B It is a liability which will only be paid upon termination of a business.

C It is a liability which will fall due for payment within twelve months of the reporting date.

D It is a liability which will fall due for payment after more than twelve months from the reporting date.

30 Which of the following statements provides a definition of an asset?

A It is a present obligation of the entity to transfer an economic resource as a result of past events

B It is a present economic resource controlled by the entity as a result of past events

C It is the excess of revenue over expenses for a period of time

D It is the net investment in the business by the proprietor

31 Which of the following statements provides a definition of a liability?

A It is a present obligation of the entity to transfer an economic resource as a result of past events

B It is a present economic resource controlled by the entity as a result of past events

C It is the excess of revenue over expenses for a period of time

D It is a decrease or outflow of economic benefits resulting from a transaction

32 Which of the following statements provides a definition of capital?

A It is the accumulated profit in the business due to the proprietor

B It is the capital introduced into the business by the proprietor

C It is the net investment in the business by the proprietor

D It is the accumulated profits less accumulated losses made by the business

33 Which of the following items correctly represents the accounting equation?

A Assets = liabilities

B Assets = Liabilities – proprietor's capital

C Assets = proprietor's capital

D Assets = Proprietor's capital + liabilities

34 Which of the following statements best explains the accounting equation?

A The accounting equation demonstrates the effect of a transaction upon the assets, liabilities and proprietor's capital of a business.

B The accounting equation demonstrates the impact a transaction on the statement of profit or loss for the year.

C The accounting equation demonstrates the effect of a transaction upon the assets and income of a business.

D The accounting equation demonstrates the effect of a transaction upon the expenses and liabilities of a business.

35 T's Sweets Co is a manufacturer and retailer of chocolates and confectionary.

Which of the following is presented as a current asset within the accounts of a business?

A The head office building of T's Sweets

B A bank balance which is overdrawn

C Manufactured chocolate products in the factory

D Trade payables

36 Which of the following transactions would have no impact upon total assets within the accounting equation?

A The injection of cash into the business by the owner

B A receipt from a credit customer paying the amount due

C The settlement of an outstanding payables to a credit supplier

D The purchase of a machine on credit

37 'A present economic resource controlled by an entity as a result of past events' is a definition of which financial accounting term?

A Materiality

B An asset

C Current value

D Income

38 Accounting systems consist of inputs, processes and outputs. Which one of the following is an input into the accounting system?

A Employee payslips

B The trial balance

C Financial statements

D Purchase invoices

39 Which one of the following is a source document for financial transactions?

A Statement of account from a supplier

B Paying in slip

C Delivery note

D Goods received note

40 Which one of the following is standing data used when processing the monthly payroll?

A Overtime hours worked by an employee

B Bonus payment awarded to selected employees

C Standard salary rates of pay

D A one-off deduction from the salary of an employee to pay for a travel season ticket

41 Identify the correct sequence of activities in an accounting system.

A Processes, followed by outputs, followed by inputs

B Outputs, followed by inputs, followed by processes

C Processes, followed by inputs, followed by outputs

D Inputs, followed by processes, followed by outputs

42 Which one of the following is not an accounting system process?

A Recording sales tax on transactions

B Calculating account balances

C Updating general ledger accounts

D The aged analysis of receivables

43 Which one of the following is an output of a computerised accounting system?

A The trial balance

B Wages rates

C Customer account details

D Summarising expenses incurred

44 Which one of the following is a definition of cloud accounting?

A Cloud accounting is a computerised accounting system

B Cloud accounting is an accounting system that enables employees to work from home

C Cloud accounting is an accounting system that enables access to accounting software and data storage hosted on remote servers so that data and information can be accessed at any time by multiple users

D Cloud accounting is an accounting system which can be used only by persons with a high level of computer-related knowledge

45 Which TWO of the following items are a component of a set of financial statements produced by a sole trader?

	Selected answer
Statement of financial position	
Bank statement	
Statement of profit or loss	
Supplier statement	

46 Which of the following statements best defines a statement of profit or loss?

A It is a summary of petty cash transactions

B It is a statement of assets and liabilities at a specific date

C It is a summary of bank receipts and payments

D It is a summary of revenue and expenses for a specified period of time

47 Which of the following statements best defines a statement of financial position?

A It is a summary of petty cash transactions

B It is a statement of assets and liabilities at a specific date

C It is a summary of bank receipts and payments

D It is a summary of revenue and expenses for a period of time

48 State whether each of the following statements is true or false.

	True/False
With a cloud accounting system, an accountant or auditor can be granted remote access to data and information they require	
With a cloud accounting system all employees are granted access to all data and information in the system	

49 What is the purpose of the journal?

A It records transactions such as amendments to the general ledger due to errors and year-end adjustments such as the depreciation charge

B It captures all credit transactions in a sequential order so that they may be summarised and the totals posted to the general ledger at appropriate intervals

C It captures all cash transactions in a sequential order so that they may be summarised and the totals posted into the general ledger

D It captures all credit transactions and all returns outwards inwards and outwards transactions in a sequential order so that they may be summarised and the totals posted to the general ledger at appropriate intervals

50 Which of the following statements best explains proprietor's capital?

A It is the amount of profit made by the business in the year

B It is the amount of accumulated profits in the business

C It is the net investment by the proprietor in the business

D It is a business liability

51 Which of the following is a valid statement in relation to the reasons to close-off the general ledger accounts and produce a trial balance?

A It is part of the double-entry accounting process

B It is a control to ensure that all transactions have been posted correctly to the correct general ledger accounts

C It is a control to ensure that that the general ledger accounts do not contain any errors

D It is a control to ensure that an equal value of debits and credits has been posted into the general ledger accounts, but that there may still be errors within those ledger accounts

52 What is the purpose of producing a trial balance?

A It confirms that there are no errors in the accounting records

B It is a preliminary step prior to preparing financial statements to ensure that there are no obvious errors or omissions within the general ledger accounts, although they may still contain errors

C It confirms whether or not the business has made a profit or loss for the year

D It confirms the proprietor's capital account balance at the end of the year

53 A trial balance consists a list of debit balances and credit balances.

Which one of the following statements is correct?

A Every debit balance represents an expense

B Assets are represented by debit balances

C Liabilities are represented by debit balances

D Income is included in the list of debit balances

54 Which two of the following general ledger accounts should have a debit balance?

	Selected answers
Petty cash	
Bank loan	
Receivables	
Proprietor's capital account	

55 What is the purpose of an entity preparing a trial balance?

A It confirms whether or not the entity made a profit or loss for the trading period

B It confirms that an equal value of debits and credits have been posted in the general ledger accounts

C It confirms that there are no errors in the trial balance

D It confirms that there are no errors in the general ledger accounts

56 Why is it good accounting practice to close-off ledger accounts and prepare a trial balance before preparing final accounts?

A It is a legal requirement to do so

B It is a requirement of the *Conceptual Framework for Financial Reporting* to do so

C It is the starting point in the process to deal with year-end adjustments, such as the annual depreciation charge, leading to preparation of the financial statements

D It confirms that, if there are errors in ledger accounts which comprise the trial balance, they are due solely to omitted transactions

THE PREPARATION OF JOURNALS AND LEDGER ACCOUNTS

57 Which one of the following states the accounting entries required to account for sales by a business which is registered to account for sales tax?

A Debit sales with net sale value credit receivables with gross invoice value and credit sales tax with sales tax value

B Debit sales with total invoice value, credit receivables with total net sale value and credit sales tax with sales tax value

C Debit receivables with total net sale value, debit sales tax with sales tax value and credit sales with gross sale value

D Debit receivables with total gross sale value, credit sales with net sale value and credit sales tax with sales tax value

58 What accounting entries are required to record goods returned inwards if the original transaction was made on credit?

A	Debit Sales revenue, and	Credit Trade payables
B	Debit Returns inwards, and	Credit Trade payables
C	Debit Returns inwards, and	Credit Trade receivables
D	Debit Trade receivables, and	Credit Returns inwards

59 What accounting entries are required to record goods returned outwards if the original transaction was made on credit?

A	Debit Payables, and	Credit Returns outwards
B	Debit Returns outwards, and	Credit Payables
C	Debit Returns outwards, and	Credit Receivables
D	Debit Receivables, and	Credit Returns outwards

60 Jo prepared the following journal adjustment:

Debit	Payables	$85
Credit	Discount	$85

Which of the following is the correct narrative for this journal entry?

A Settlement discount allowed relating to payables

B Trade discount received relating to payables

C Settlement discount received relating to payables

D Trade discount allowed relating to payables

61 Andi started a taxi business by transferring a car, valued at $5,000, into the business. What accounting entries are required to record the transfer of the car into the business?

A	Debit	Capital	Credit	Motor vehicle
B	Debit	Motor vehicle	Credit	Drawings
C	Debit	Motor vehicle	Credit	Capital
D	Debit	Motor vehicle	Credit	Bank

62 Which of the following is the correct journal entry to write off an irrecoverable debt?

A	Debit	Sales	Credit	irrecoverable debts
B	Debit	Irrecoverable debts	Credit	Bank
C	Debit	Receivables	Credit	Irrecoverable debts
D	Debit	Irrecoverable debts	Credit	Receivables

63 Barclay had accounts receivable of $42,750 and $44,325 at 1 January 20X8 and 31 December 20X8 respectively.

During 20X8, cash sales of $265,000 and credit sales of $362,750 were made, contras with payables amounted to $18,750 and discounts received totalled 22,685. Irrecoverable debts of $8,640 were written off during 20X8 and Barclay wishes to retain its allowance for receivables at 5% of total receivables.

What was the cash received by Barclay from credit customers during the year?

A $336,935

B $352,535

C $329,850

D $333,785

64 Wilson has returned goods which had been purchased from a supplier on credit. What journal entry should Wilson make in the general ledger to record this transaction?

A	Debit	Purchase returns	Credit	Payables
B	Debit	Payables	Credit	Bank
C	Debit	Bank	Credit	Payables
D	Debit	Payables	Credit	Purchase returns

65 Which of the following statements relating to the journal is true?

A The journal records all bank and cash transactions

B The journal records the profit or loss made for the year

C The journal records all accounting transactions

D The journal records all credit sales transactions

66 What is a ledger account?

A A ledger account is a record of all transactions that were initially recorded in the bank general ledger account

B A ledger account is a record of all transactions that affect the statement of profit or loss

C A ledger account is a record of all transactions relating to a particular item in accordance with the principles of double-entry bookkeeping during an accounting period

D A ledger account is a record of all transactions that occurred during an accounting period

67 What is the general ledger?

A The general ledger a record of assets and liabilities of the business

B The general ledger is a record of all amounts owed to individual suppliers and all amounts owed by individual customers

C The general ledger contains the statement of profit or loss and the statement of financial position

D The general ledger contains all of the individual ledger accounts used by a business

68 What is the purpose of a ledger account?

A It enables a business to classify record and summarise transactions in an orderly and consistent manner

B It enables a business to identify the value of assets and liabilities at any point in time

C It enables a business to determine whether a business made a profit or a loss during an accounting period

D It enables a business to determine the capital account balance of the proprietor at any point in time

69 The following account was extracted from the general ledger of Ali:

Purchases

	$		$
Purchases – Jan	4,700	Journal 25	1,327
Purchases – Feb	3,387		
Purchases – Mar	5,471		
	______		______
	______		______

What is the balance carried down on this ledger account?

$	*Debit/Credit *Delete which does not apply

70 The following account was extracted from the general ledger of Ali:

Sales account

	$		$
Journal	854	Balance brought forward	18,471
		Sales – Jun	4,200
		Sales – Jul	5,387
		Sales – Aug	7,935
	______		______
	______		______

What was the balance brought down on this ledger account?

$	*Debit/Credit *Delete which does not apply

RECORDING TRANSACTIONS AND EVENTS

71 **Which of the following is the correct formula to calculate cost of sales?**

A Purchases – Opening inventory – Closing inventory

B Purchases + Opening inventory + Closing inventory

C Purchases – Opening inventory + Closing inventory

D Purchases + Opening inventory – Closing inventory

72 Acme Co wants to return goods purchased on credit from a supplier which cost $300.

Which of the following is the correct double-entry for Acme Co to record the return of goods to the supplier?

A Debit Trade payables $300, and Credit Purchases $300

B Debit Purchases $300, and Credit Trade payables $300

C Debit Trade payables $300, and Credit Returns outwards $300

D Debit Purchases $300, and Credit Returns outwards $300

73 Wolf Co issued a sales invoice to the value of $450 to a customer who paid immediately for the goods.

What accounting entries should Wolf Co make to record this transaction?

A Debit Receivables $450, and Credit Sales $450

B Debit Bank $450, and Credit Receivables $450

C Debit Sales $450, and Credit Bank $450

D Debit Bank $450, and Credit Sales $450

74 A credit customer returned goods to Fox Co as they were found to be damaged upon receipt. The value of the returned goods was $281.

What accounting entries should Fox Co make to record this transaction?

A	Debit Receivables $281, and	Credit	Sales $281
B	Debit Returns inwards $281, and	Credit	Receivables $281
C	Debit Sales $281, and	Credit	Returns inwards $281
D	Debit Returns inwards $281, and	Credit	Bank $281

75 Coyote Co made a purchase of goods from a local warehouse which cost $85. The payment was made immediately by using a business debit card.

Which of the following is the correct double-entry for Coyote Co to record the purchase of goods?

A	Debit Purchases $85, and	Credit	Bank $85
B	Debit Purchases $85, and	Credit	Trade payables $85
C	Debit Purchases $85, and	Credit	Petty cash $85
D	Debit Trade payables $85, and	Credit	Purchases $85

76 Ibex Co sold goods on credit to a customer which had a value of $125.

What accounting entries should Ibex Co make to record this transaction?

A	Debit Bank $125, and	Credit	Sales $125
B	Debit Inventory $125, and	Credit	Sales $125
C	Debit Receivables $125, and	Credit	Bank $125
D	Debit Receivables $125, and	Credit	Sales $125

77 Bear Co made a purchase of goods on credit from a supplier which cost $273.

Which of the following is the correct double-entry for Bear Co to record the purchase of goods?

A	Debit Purchases $273, and	Credit	Trade payables $273
B	Debit Inventory $273, and	Credit	Trade payables $273
C	Debit Purchases $273, and	Credit	Bank $273
D	Debit Purchases $273, and	Credit	Inventory $273

78 Raven Co is operating a newly-established business.

When, if ever, should Raven Co account or sales tax?

A At some point within the first year of trading

B As soon as it is registered with the tax authority to do so

C As soon as it makes a sales to a credit customer

D As soon as it makes a cash purchase of goods for resale

79 Vulture Co is operating a business which is registered to account for sales tax. Vulture Co operates in a country which has more than one rate of sales tax.

What rate of sales tax should Vulture apply to its sales?

A The highest of the sales tax rates currently in force

B The lowest of the sales tax rates currently in force

C The rate applicable to each individual sale of goods concerned

D The average rate of the sales tax rates currently in force

80 Hawk Co operates a business which is registered to account for sales tax. During the sales tax return period for the three months to 30 June 20X5, Hawk Co had sales tax inputs which exceeded sales tax inputs.

What is the sales tax position of Hawk Co?

A Hawk Co will receive a repayment of net input tax

B Hawk Co will need to pay net input tax to the tax authority

C The tax authority will decide what amount of sales tax Hawk Co will need to pay

D The tax authority will decided what amount of sales tax Hawk Co will be repaid

81 Falcon Co is registered to account for sales tax. Falcon Co makes sales of goods which are zero-rated for sales tax purposes.

What is the sales tax position of Falcon Co?

A In effect, it is outside the scope of the sales tax system and should withdraw from the sales tax system

B It can nether charge, nor recover, sales tax on its transactions

C It charges a zero rate of sales tax on its sales and cannot recover the sales tax suffered on purchases

D It charges a zero rate of sales tax on its sales and can recover sales tax suffered on purchases

82 Peacock Co is registered to account for sales tax. For the sales tax return period ended 31 July 20X2, Peacock made several errors on the return submitted to the tax authority, resulting in it paying less sales tax than it should have paid.

What is the sales tax position of Peacock Co?

A It should advise the tax authority as soon as possible and pay the additional amount due and may be liable to pay interest and penalties

B Nothing can be done as it is too late to do anything about it

C It should advise the tax authority as soon as possible and pay the additional amount due

D It should correct the errors made in the next sales tax return submitted to the tax authority

83 Andi's trial balance at 31 October 20X7 includes the following balances:

	$
Machinery at cost	85,800
Accumulated depreciation on machinery	21,750
Receivables	42,650
Receivables allowance	1,570
Bank overdraft	6,470
Inventory at 1 November 20X6	21,650

Andi's inventory at 31 October 20X7 is valued at $22,300.

What value should be reported for current assets in Andi's statement of financial position at 31 October 20X7?

A $62,730

B $63,380

C $64,950

D $69,850

84 Jak is preparing the trial balance at 31 October 20X7. At 1 November 20X6 Jak had an accrual of $297 for telephone expenses. During the year to 31 October 20X7 Jak paid invoices for telephone charges up to 31 October 20X7 of $4,570.

What debit balance should Jake include in the trial balance at 31 October 20X7 for telephone expenses?

$

The following information relates to questions 85 and 86:

The total amount owed to Bao by customers at 30 November 20X7 was $78,600. Bao decided that a balance of $600 should be written off as it is irrecoverable and that, based upon a review of receivables, a specific allowance equivalent to 1.5% of the remaining receivables balance is required. Bao's receivables allowance at 1 December 20X6 was $1,200.

Note: in the exam, all questions will be independent, and not based on a common scenario.

---

85 Bao made the entry in the irrecoverable debts expense account to write off the irrecoverable balance.

What other entry does Bao need to make?

A A debit entry in the sales account

B A credit entry in the sales account

C A debit entry in the receivables account

D A credit entry in the receivables account

86 How should the movement in the receivables allowance be reflected in the statement of profit or loss?

A A credit of $21

B A charge of $21

C A credit of $30

D A charge of $30

87 A business has capital of $10,000. Which of the following asset and liability figures could appear in this business' statement of financial position?

A	Assets	$6,000	Liabilities	$16,000
B	Assets	$6,000	Liabilities	$4,000
C	Assets	$10,000	Liabilities	$10,000
D	Assets	$14,000	Liabilities	$4,000

88 Which of the following is the correct double-entry to record the return of goods which had been purchased on credit by a business?

A	Debit Purchase returns, and	Credit	Purchases
B	Debit Purchases, and	Credit	Payables
C	Debit Purchase returns, and	Credit	Inventory
D	Debit Payables, and	Credit	Purchase returns

89 A sole trader had opening capital of $10,000 and closing capital of $4,500. During the period, the owner introduced capital of $4,000 and withdrew $8,000 for own use.

What loss did the business make for the year?

$

90 At 31 May 20X7 Bobbie's trial balance included the following items:

	$
Inventory at 1 June 20X6	23,856
Receivables	55,742
Payables	32,165
Bank overdraft	5,855
Loan due for repayment in 20X9	15,000

What was the value of Bobbie's current liabilities at 31 May 20X7?

$

91 A business returned goods that had a net value of $800 to a supplier. What would be the debit to the payables general ledger account if sales tax is payable at a rate of 10% by the business?

A $720.00

B $800.00

C $880.00

D $969.70

92 A summary of the transactions of Ramsgate Co, which is registered to account for sales tax at 15%, showed the following for the month of August 20X9.

Outputs	$60,000 (exclusive of sales tax)
Inputs	$46,000 (inclusive of sales tax)

At the beginning of the period Ramsgate Co owed $3,400 to the government tax authority, and during the period $2,600 was paid to the tax authority.

What was the amount owed to the government tax authorities at the end of the accounting period?

$

The following information relates to questions 93 to 95

The following information was extracted from the books of Max at 31 December 20X8:

	$
Sales	18,955
Cost of sales	11,334
Salaries and wages	2,447
Motor expenses	664
Rent	456
Rates	120
Insurance	146
Packing expenses	276
Lighting and heating expenses	665
Sundry expenses	115
Motor vehicles	2,400
Fixtures and fittings	600
Inventory as at 31 December 20X8	4,998
Receivables	4,577
Payables	3,045
Cash at bank	3,876
Cash in hand	120
Capital	10,794

Note: in the exam, all questions will be independent, and not based on a common scenario.

93 **What is the current liabilities figure in the statement of financial position at 31 December 20X8?**

$

94 **What is the non-current assets figure at 31 December 20X8?**

$

95 **What is the net profit for the year ended 31 December 20X8?**

$

96 **How is closing inventory recorded in the accounting records?**

A By a debit to inventory and a credit to profit or loss

B By a debit to profit or loss and a credit to inventory

C By a debit to inventory and a credit to purchases

D By writing the figure in a note beneath the trial balance

97 **How is the closing balance on accounts receivable included in the statement of financial position?**

A By a debit to accounts receivable and a credit to statement of financial position

B By a debit to statement of financial position and a credit to accounts receivable

C By a debit to statement of financial position

D By including the total in the statement of financial position, the balance on accounts receivable remaining unaffected

98 Gulzar received goods which cost $250 from Baz on credit terms and Gulzar subsequently paid by cheque. Gulzar then discovered that the goods were faulty, returned the goods and cancelled the cheque before it was recorded and cashed by Baz.

What accounting entries should Gulzar use when recording cancellation of the cheque in the accounting records?

A	Debit Accounts payable, and	Credit Returns outwards
B	Debit Bank, and	Credit Returns outwards
C	Debit Bank, and	Credit Accounts payable
D	Debit Accounts payable, and	Credit Returns outwards

99 **Which of the following is a bank overdraft an example of?**

A An asset

B A liability

C Revenue

D Expense

100 Gunjan, who is a sole trader, made a profit of $22,860 in the year to 30 November 20X5. During the year Gunjan's drawings were $16,890. At 1 December 20X4 the balance on Gunjan's capital account was $68,920.

What is the balance on Gunjan's capital account at 30 November 20X5?

$

101 At 30 November 20X5 Jez had a bank loan of $8,500 and a balance of $678 in hand in the bank account.

How should these amounts be recorded in Jez's opening trial balance at 1 December 20X5?

A Debit $7,822

B Credit $7,822

C Credit $8,500 and Debit $678

D Debit $8,500 and Credit $678

102 During May 20X7, Sam's purchases were $126,500, and sales were $150,000. Sam's gross profit margin is 20% of sales. The value of inventory at 1 May 20X7 was $12,500.

What was the value of Sam's inventory at 31 May 20X7?

$

103 At 31 May 20X6 Dex's capital balance was $96,578. During the year to 31 May 20X7, Dex made drawings of 25,764. At 31 May 20X7 Dex had a capital account balance of $104,864.

What was Dex's profit for the year ended 31 May 20X7?

$

104 A business borrowed $1,700 from its bank, and used the cash to buy a new computer.

How is the accounting equation affected following these transactions?

	Assets	**Liabilities**
A	Unchanged	Decreased
B	Unchanged	Increased
C	Increased	Increased
D	Increased	Decreased

105 In the year to 31 May 20X6, Veda paid $2,500 for property repairs. Veda's bookkeeper treated this as asset expenditure.

What is the effect of this error on Vida's profit for the year to 31 May 20X6, and the value of assets at that date?

	Profit	Assets
A	Understated	Overstated
B	Understated	Understated
C	Overstated	Overstated
D	Overstated	Understated

106 Eddie estimated that, at 31 May 20X6, the business had the following assets and liabilities:

	$
Non-current assets	33,750
Inventory	4,845
Receivables	11,248
Payables	9,633
Bank overdraft	539

Upon checking, you note that Eddie also has a prepayment for rent of $520.

What is Eddie's capital account balance at 31 May 20X6?

$

107 At 31 October 20X6 Jaime had an outstanding balance of $24,000 on the bank loan account. The terms of the loan require Jaime to repay $400 on the first day of each month.

How should the loan be reported in Jaime's statement of financial position at 31 October 20X6?

	Current liability	Non-current liability
A	nil	$24,000
B	$24,000	nil
C	$19,200	$4,800
D	$4,800	$19,200

108 At 31 October 20X6 Kim's trial balance included the following balances:

	$
Machinery at cost	12,890
Accumulated depreciation	8,950
Inventory	5,754
Receivables	11,745
Payables	7,830
Bank overdraft	1,675
Cash at bank	150

What was the carrying amount of Kim's current assets at 31 October 20X6?

$

109 At 1 May 20X7 Heng had an opening accrual of $353 for motor expenses. During the year to 30 April 20X8 Heng paid invoices for motor expenses with a total value of $4,728. Heng has no closing accrual or prepayment at 30 April 20X8.

What balance should Heng include in the trial balance for motor expenses?

A $4,375 debit

B $4,375 credit

C $5,081 debit

D $5,081 credit

110 The balance on Vibhuti's payables' general ledger account is $31,554. Vibhuti subsequently discovered that the following items were not recorded:

- a settlement discount of $53 received from a supplier; and
- a supplier's invoice for $622.

What amount should be reported for payables in Vibhuti's statement of financial position?

A $30,879

B $30,985

C $32,123

D $32,229

111 **Which of the following is the correct double-entry to record the purchase of goods on credit by a business?**

A	Debit Trade payables, and	Credit	Purchases
B	Debit Purchases, and	Credit	Trade receivables
C	Debit Trade receivables, and	Credit	Revenue
D	Debit Purchases, and	Credit	Trade payables

112 Which of the following is the correct journal entry to record a credit note issued to a customer who returned goods, having purchased them on credit?

A	Debit Sales returns, and	Credit	Cash
B	Debit Cash, and	Credit	Sales returns
C	Debit Trade receivables, and	Credit	Sales returns
D	Debit Sales returns, and	Credit	Trade receivables

113 Kim's trial balance at 30 September 20X4 included the following balances:

	$
Machinery at cost	96,400
Accumulated depreciation on machinery	23,500
Trade receivables	48,325
Receivables allowance	1,840
Bank overdraft	7,360
Inventory at 1 October 20X3	23,200

Kim's inventory at 30 September 20X4 was valued at $25,700.

What carrying amount should be reported for current assets at 30 September 20X4?

$

114 Harsha's trial balance at 30 June 20X6 included the following balances:

	$
Trade payables	38,975
Accumulated depreciation on machinery	24,200
Trade receivables	48,325
Allowance for receivables	3,200
Bank overdraft	6,125
Bank loan due for repayment 30 June 20X9	23,200

What carrying amount should be reported for current liabilities in Harsha's statement of financial position at 30 June 20X6?

$

115 Hemal is preparing the trial balance at 31 March 20X3. At 1 April 20X2 Hemal had an accrual of $327 for heat and light charges. During the year to 31 March 20X3 Hemal paid invoices for heat and light charges up to 31 March 20X3 of $8,750.

What balance should Hemal include in the trial balance at 31 March 20X3 for heat and light charges?

A $9,077 debit

B $8,423 credit

C $8,423 debit

D $9,077 credit

The following information relates to questions 116 and 117:

The total amount owed to Maz by credit customers at 31 December 20X5 was $83,200. Maz decided that a balance of $1,825 should be written off as it is irrecoverable, and that, following a review of accounts receivables balances, an allowance of $6,510 was required at 31 December 20X5. The allowance for receivables at 1 January 20X5 was $8,200.

Note: in the exam, all questions will be independent, and not based on a common scenario.

116 Maz has made the correct entry in the expense account to write off the irrecoverable balance. What other accounting entry does Maz need to make?

A A debit entry in the sales account

B A credit entry in the sales account

C A debit entry in the receivables account

D A credit entry in the receivables account

117 How is the movement in the allowance for receivables be reflected in the statement of profit or loss?

A A credit of $1,544

B A charge of $1,544

C A credit of $1,690

D A charge of $1,690

118 A business had total assets of $25,000. Which of the following capital and liability figures could appear in this business' statement of financial position?

A	Capital	$10,000	Liabilities	$35,000
B	Capital	$10,000	Liabilities	$15,000
C	Capital	$18,000	Liabilities	$43,000
D	Capital	$40,000	Liabilities	$15,000

119 A sole trader had opening capital of $18,000 and closing capital of $6,900. During the accounting period, the owner introduced capital of $6,000 and withdrew $10,000 for own use.

What was the loss for the accounting period?

$

120 West returned goods to a supplier that had a net value of $560. What was the value of the debit entry to the payables account in West's accounting records if sales tax is payable at a rate of 20%?

$

121 A summary of the transactions of Kent, who is registered for sales tax at 20%, shows the following for the month of July 20X1:

Outputs $90,000 (exclusive of sales tax), and Inputs $75,000 (inclusive of sales tax).

At the beginning of the month Kent owed $4,275 to the government tax authority, and during the month Kent paid $4,100 to the tax authority.

What was the amount owing to the government tax authority at the end of the month?

$

The following information relates to questions 122 to 125:

The following information was extracted from the books of Les at 30 June 20X4:

	$
Sales	21,370
Cost of sales	12,413
Salaries and wages	3,560
Motor expenses	572
Rent	600
Rates	150
Lighting and heating expenses	702
Sundry expenses	113
Motor vehicles	7,200
Fixtures and fittings	1,000
Inventory as at 30 June 20X4	5,243
Receivables	6,715
Payables	3,115
Cash in hand	115
Overdraft	350
Capital	13,548

Note: in the exam, all questions will be independent, and not based on a common scenario.

---

122 **What carrying amount for current liabilities should be included in the statement of financial position at 30 June 20X4?**

A $3,115

B $3,465

C $3,345

D $2,765

123 **What carrying amount for non-current assets should be included in the statement of financial position as at 30 June 20X4?**

$

124 **What was the net profit for the year ended 30 June 20X4?**

$

125 What carrying amount for current assets should be included in the statement of financial position as at 30 June 20X4?

A $11,858

B $11,958

C $11,723

D $12,073

126 What are the accounting entries required to record goods returned outwards?

A Debit sales account and credit returns outwards account

B Debit returns outwards account and credit receivables account

C Debit returns outwards account and credit payables account

D Debit payables account and credit returns outwards account

127 Oxford Co had a total accounts receivable balance of $84,700 at 1 May 20X6 and $82,500 at 30 June 20X7. During the year ended 30 June 20X7, there were cash sales of $86,400 and cash received from receivables of $564,250. During the year ended 30 June 20X7, contras with the payables general ledger account amounted to $8,300 and discounts received totalled $17,260. Irrecoverable receivables of $12,650 were written off and Oxford Co wishes to have an allowance for receivables of $3,300 at 30 June 20X7.

What was the value of credit sales made in the year ended 30 June 20X2?

$

128 A trial balance consists of a list of debit balances and credit balances.

Which of the following statements is correct?

A Every debit balance represents an asset

B Assets are represented by credit balances

C Liabilities are represented by credit balances

D Income is included in the list of debit balances

129 During June 20X9, Ina's purchases were $160,000, and sales were $180,000. Ina's gross profit is 10% of sales. The value of Ina's inventory at 1 June 20X9 was $20,000.

What was the value of Ina's inventory at 30 June 20X9?

$

130 At 1 May 20X5 Matti's capital balance was $89,627. During the year to 30 April 20X6, Matti's profit for the year was $32,678. At 30 April 20X6 Matti's capital balance was $98,473.

What were Matti's drawings for the year ended 30 April 20X6?

$

131 In the year ended 31 January 20X5, Jehan paid $3,700 for new fixtures and fittings. Jehan's bookkeeper treated this item as an expense.

What is the effect of this error on Jehan's profit for the year to 31 May 20X6, and the value of assets at that date?

	Profit	Assets
A	Understated	Overstated
B	Understated	Understated
C	Overstated	Overstated
D	Overstated	Understated

132 Ellis estimated that, at 31 August 20X4, the business had the following assets and liabilities:

	$
Non-current assets	33,750
Inventory	4,845
Trade receivables	11,248
Trade payables	9,633
Bank overdraft	539

Upon checking this information, you note that Ellis also had an accrual for rent of £750 which had not been accounted for.

What was the balance on Ellis' capital account at 31 August 20X4?

$

133 Which of the following are the correct accounting entries to record the sale of goods on credit by a business?

A	Debit Revenue, and	Credit	Trade receivables
B	Debit Purchases, and	Credit	Trade receivables
C	Debit Trade receivables, and	Credit	Revenue
D	Debit Purchases, and	Credit	Trade payables

134 At 31 December 20X5, a sole trader had a closing capital balance of $15,250. During the year ended 31 December 20X5, the sole trader introduced capital of $3,800 and withdrew $7,300 for own use. The business made a profit for the year ended 31 December 20X5 of $8,500.

What was the opening capital balance at 1 January 20X5?

$

135 At 31 May 20X7 Vic's trial balance included the following items:

	$
Inventory at 1 June 20X6	23,056
Trade receivables	55,742
Trade payables	32,165
Petty cash balance	100
Bank overdraft	5,855
Fixtures and fittings	15,000

Based upon the available information, what was the value of Vic's current assets at 31 May 20X7?

$

136 ABC Co sold goods with a list price of $1,000 to Smith which was subject to trade discount of 5% and early settlement discount of 4% if the invoice was paid within 7 days. The normal credit period available to credit customers is 30 days from invoice date. Based upon past experience, Smith has never taken advantage of early settlement terms and has always paid after 30 days.

If Smith subsequently pays within 7 days and is eligible for the settlement discount, what accounting entries should be made by ABC Co to record settlement of the amount outstanding?

A Debit Cash $950, Debit Revenue $50 and Credit Trade receivables $1,000

B Debit Cash $950, Credit Revenue $38 and Credit Trade receivables $912

C Debit Cash $912, Debit Revenue $38 and Credit Trade receivables $950

D Debit Cash $912, and Credit Trade receivables $912

137 ABC Co sold goods with a list price of $2,500 to Jones which was subject to trade discount of 5% and early settlement discount of 4% if the invoice was paid within 7 days. The normal credit period available to credit customers is 30 days from invoice date. Based upon past experience, Jones always takes advantage of early settlement terms.

If Jones subsequently pays within 7 days and is eligible for the settlement discount, what accounting entries should be made by ABC Co to record settlement of the amount outstanding?

A Debit Cash $2,280, Debit Revenue $95 and Credit Trade receivables $2,375

B Debit Cash $2,280 and Credit Trade receivables $2,280

C Debit Cash $2,375, Debit Revenue $125 and Credit Trade receivables $2,500

D Debit Cash $2,500, and Credit Trade receivables $2,500

138 ABC Co sold goods with a list price of $4,500 to Black which was subject to trade discount of 5% and early settlement discount of 4% if the invoice was paid within 7 days. The normal credit period available to credit customers is 30 days from invoice date. Based upon past experience, Black always takes advantage of early settlement terms.

If, on this occasion, Black subsequently pays after 7 days and is not eligible for the settlement discount, what accounting entries should be made by ABC Co to record settlement of the amount outstanding?

A Debit Cash $4,104, Debit Revenue $396 and Credit Trade receivables $4,500

B Debit Cash $4,275, Debit Revenue $171 and Credit Trade receivables $4,104

C Debit Cash $4,275 and Credit Trade receivables $4,275

D Debit Cash $4,275, Credit Trade receivables $4,104 and Credit Revenue $171

139 ABC Co sold goods with a list price of $3,700 to White which was subject to trade discount of 5% and early settlement discount of 4% if the invoice was paid within 7 days. The normal credit period available to credit customers is 30 days from invoice date. Based upon past experience, White does not normally pay early to take advantage of early settlement terms.

If, as expected, White subsequently pays after 30 days, what accounting entries should be made by ABC Co to record settlement of the amount outstanding?

A Debit Cash $3,515, and Credit Trade receivables $3,515

B Debit Cash $3,515, Credit Discount received $140.60 and Credit Trade receivables $3,374.40

C Debit Cash $3,374.40 and Credit Trade receivables $3,374.40

D Debit Cash $3,515, Debit Revenue $185 and Credit Trade receivables $3,700

140 ABC Co sold goods with a list price of $1,400 to Green which was subject to trade discount of 4% and early settlement discount of 5% if the invoice was paid within 7 days. The normal credit period available to credit customers is 30 days from invoice date. Based upon past experience, Green has always taken advantage of early settlement terms and has always paid within 7 days.

If, on this occasion, Green subsequently pays after 30 days, what accounting entries should be made by ABC Co to record settlement of the amount outstanding?

A Debit Cash $1,344.00, Credit Trade receivables $1,276.80 and Credit Revenue $67.20

B Debit Cash $1,400 Credit Trade receivables $1,400

C Debit Cash $1,344 and Credit Trade receivables $1,344

D Debit Cash $1,276.80, and Credit Trade receivables $1,276.80

INVENTORIES

141 Lazim recently commenced trading. The materials Lazim uses in the business are subject to regular price rises. Lazim is unsure how to value inventory and is trying to decide whether to use 'first in, first out' (FIFO), or continuous weighted average.

Which of the following statements is correct?

A Lazim's profit will be unaffected by the method of inventory valuation

B FIFO will lead to the higher reported profit

C Continuous weighted average will lead to the higher reported profit

D The profit will be more accurate if FIFO is used

142 You are preparing the final accounts for a business. The cost of the items in closing inventory is $41,875. This includes some items which cost $1,960 and which were damaged in transit. You have estimated that it will cost $360 to repair the items, and that the items could then be sold for $1,200.

What was the correct inventory valuation for inclusion in the final accounts?

$

143 Kranti uses the first in, first out method of inventory valuation. At 1 May 20X8 Kranti had 60 units in inventory at a total value of $1,320. The movements in inventory in May 20X8 were as follows:

Receipts	14 May	120 units at $22.20
	26 May	150 units at $22.30
Sales	18 May	90 units
	28 May	80 units

What was the value of Kranti's inventory at 31 May 20X8?

$

144 Manasi uses the periodic weighted average method of inventory valuation. At 1 August 20X6 Manasi had 60 units in inventory at a total value of $1,320. The inventory movements during August 20X6 were as follows:

Receipts	14 Aug	120 units at $22.50 per unit
	26 Aug	150 units at $23.36 per unit
Sales	18 Aug	90 units
	28 Aug	80 units

What was the value of Manasi's inventory at 31 August 20X6?

$

145 Kuntal the continuous weighted average cost method of inventory valuation. At 1 February 20X4 Kuntal had 60 units in inventory at a total value of $1,320. The inventory movements during February 20X4 were as follows:

Receipts	14 Feb	180 units at $23.00 per unit
Sales	18 Feb	90 units at $30.00 per unit

What was the value of Kuntal's inventory at 28 February 20X4?

A $3,300.00

B $3,390.00

C $3,412.50

D $3,450.00

146 Drew uses the continuous weighted average cost method of inventory valuation. At 1 April 20X5 Drew had 120 units in inventory at a unit cost of $22.00. The inventory movements during April 20X5 were as follows:

Receipts	15 Apr	360 units at $23.00 per unit
Sales	25 Apr	300 units at $32.00 per unit

What was Drew's cost of sales for the month of April 20X5?

$

147 An item of inventory was purchased for $500. It is expected to be sold for $1,200 although $250 will need to be spent on it in order to achieve the sale. To replace the same item of inventory would cost $650.

At what value should this item of inventory be valued in the financial statements?

$

148 Ajay's financial year end is 30 June 20X6. However, the annual inventory count took place on 7 July 20X6. The inventory value on that date was $38,950. During the period from 30 June 20X6 to 7 July 20X6, the following transactions took place:

Sales	$6,500
Purchases	$4,250

Sales are made at a mark-up on cost of 25%.

What was Ajay's inventory valuation at 30 June 20X6?

A $36,700

B $41,200

C $39,900

D $38,000

149 Jital is a book wholesaler. On each sale, commission of 4% is payable to the selling agent. The following information is available in respect of total inventories at the year-end of three of the most popular titles:

	Cost	**Selling price**
	$	$
Henry VII – Shakespeare	2,280	2,900
Dissuasion – Jane Armstrong-Siddeley	4,080	4,000
Pilgrim's Painful Progress – John Bunion	1,280	1,300

What was the total value of these items of inventory in Jital's statement of financial position?

A $7,368

B $7,400

C $7,560

D $7,640

150 An organisation had inventory at 1 July of 15 units purchased at a unit cost of $3.00. The following inventory subsequent movements occurred:

3 July 20X4	5 units sold at $3.30 each
8 July 20X4	10 units bought at $3.50 each
12 July 20X4	8 units sold at $4.00 each

At what valuation will closing inventory be included in the financial statements at 31 July, using the first in, first out, method of inventory valuation?

A $31.50

B $36.00

C $39.00

D $41.00

151 Mehal has closing inventory which cost $38,750. This includes some damaged items which cost $3,660. It will cost Mehal $450 to repair these. Mehal will be able to sell them for $1,500 after the repairs are completed.

What is the correct value of Mehal closing inventory?

A $35,090

B $36,140

C $36,590

D $38,750

152 Which method of inventory valuation is used when issues are assumed to be taken from inventory in the order in which they were received?

A Net realisable value

B First in, first out

C Periodic weighted average

D Continuous weighted average

153 When Yanni prepared the draft accounts, closing inventory at a value of $21,870 was included. Yanni has just discovered that some items valued at $2,150 had not been included in the valuation.

How will net profit and net assets be affected when the inventory valuation is corrected?

	Net profit	Net assets
A	Reduced by $2,150	Reduced by £2,150
B	Reduced by $2,140	Increased by $2,150
C	Increased by $2,150	Reduced by $2,150
D	Increased by $2,150	Increased by $2,150

154 Nartan made a mistake when performing calculations which resulted in the value of closing inventory at 30 April 20X4 being overstated by $900. The value was calculated correctly at 30 April 20X5.

What was the effect of the error on the profit reported in Nartan's accounts for each of the two years?

	20X4	20X5
A	Overstated by $900	Not affected
B	Overstated by $900	Understated by $900
C	Understated by $900	Not affected
D	Understated by $900	Overstated by $900

155 Niral is an antiques dealer. Niral's inventory includes a clock which cost $15,800. Niral expects to spend $700 on repairing the clock which will mean that it could then be sold for $26,000.

At what value should the clock be included in Niral's inventory?

$

156 LMN Co has just published its financial statements, which show a gross profit for the year of $6.5 million. A major error in the inventory valuation has just been discovered. The opening inventory was overstated by $1.3 million, and the closing inventory has been understated by $1.6 million.

What should be LMN Co's correct gross profit for the year?

$

157 What is the unit cost of the following item?

	$
Raw materials	5.00
Labour	3.00
Manufacturing overheads	1.00
Variable administrative overheads	2.50

A $5.00

B $8.00

C $9.00

D $11.50

158 Daz made an error when calculating the value of closing inventory, which resulted in an overvaluation of inventory.

How will Daz's net profit for the year and net assets at the end of the year be affected by this error?

	Net profit	**Net assets**
A	Overstated	Understated
B	Overstated	Overstated
C	Understated	Understated
D	Understated	Overstated

159 What is the net realisable value of the following item?

	$
Selling price	20.00
Packaging costs	2.00
Delivery costs	3.00
Licence fee paid after delivery	2.50

$

160 Diesel fuel included in the inventory of an entity at 1 November 20X7 was $12,500 and, of this, invoices were still to be received for deliveries which cost $1,700. During the year to 31 October 20X8, diesel fuel bills of $85,400 were paid, and a delivery of diesel fuel costing $1,300 had yet to be invoiced. At 31 October 20X8, the inventory of diesel fuel was valued at $9,800.

What amount is to be charged to the statement of profit or loss for the year to 31 October 20X8 for diesel fuel?

$

161 Suresh & Co sells three products – Basic, Super and Luxury. The following information was available at the year-end:

	Basic	Super	Luxury
	$ per unit	**$ per unit**	**$ per unit**
Original cost	6	9	18
Estimated selling price	9	12	15
Selling and distribution costs	1	4	5
	Units	**Units**	**Units**
Units held	200	250	150

What should be the valuation of inventory at the end of the year?

$

162 **In times of rising prices, what will be the effect upon profit and closing inventory valuation using the first in, first out method of inventory valuation in comparison to the average cost method of inventory valuation?**

A A higher profit and a lower closing inventory value

B A higher profit and a higher closing inventory value

C A lower profit and a lower closing inventory value

D A lower profit and a higher inventory value

163 Arlo valued inventory at 30 June 20X1 at its cost of $22,960. This included some items which cost $1,950 which have been difficult to sell. Arlo intends to have these items repacked at a cost of $400 and then expects to sell them for $900.

What was the value of closing inventory in Arlo's accounts at 30 June 20X1?

$

164 At 30 November 20X1 Kaz's inventory was valued at its cost of $22,700. This includes items costing $1,300 which have been superseded by an updated design. Kaz will be able to sell these items through an agent for $700. The agent's commission will be payable on this transaction at 10% of selling price.

What was the value of closing inventory on 30 November 20X1?

$

165 Lee uses the periodic weighted average method of inventory valuation. At 1 November 20X7 Lee had 60 units in inventory at a total value of $1,320. The inventory movements during August 20X6 were as follows:

Receipts	14 Nov	150 units at $20.00 per unit
	26 Nov	100 units at $25.00 per unit
Sales	18 Nov	80 units sold for $30 per unit
	28 Nov	90 units sold for $30 per unit

What was the value of Lee's inventory at 30 November 20X7?

A $6,820

B $3,740

C $3,080

D $1,760

166 Dani uses the continuous weighted average cost method of inventory valuation. At 1 April 20X9 Dani had 50 units in inventory at a total value of $815. The inventory movements during February 20X4 were as follows:

Receipts	14 Apr	270 units at $19.50 per unit
Sales	18 Apr	180 units at $35.00 per unit

What was the cost of goods sold by Dani for the month of April 20X9?

$

167 **What is the double-entry to record the value of inventory withdrawn from the business by the proprietor for own use?**

A Debit Drawings, and Credit Capital

B Debit Purchases, and Credit Drawings

C Debit Inventory (Statement of FP), and Credit Inventory (Statement of P&L)

D Debit Drawings, and Credit Purchases

168 During the process to prepare the final accounts, the proprietor identified that several items of closing inventory had been valued incorrectly. A cost of $100 per unit had been used, rather than the correct cost of $70 per unit.

What accounting entries are required to correct this error?

A Debit Inventory (Statement of P&L), and Credit Purchases

B Debit Inventory (Statement of P&L), and Credit Inventory (Statement of FP)

C Debit Inventory (Statement of FP), and Credit Inventory (Statement of P&L)

D Debit Purchases (Statement of FP), and Credit Inventory

169 What is the double-entry to record the value of closing inventory in the final accounts of an entity?

A Debit Inventory (Statement of P&L), and Credit Purchases

B Debit Inventory (Statement of P&L), and Credit Inventory (Statement of FP)

C Debit Inventory (Statement of FP), and Credit Inventory (Statement of P&L)

D Debit Purchases (Statement of FP), and Credit Inventory

NON-CURRENT ASSETS AND DEPRECIATION

170 What is the accounting concept that specifies non-current assets should be valued at cost less accumulated depreciation, rather than at their enforced saleable value?

A Net realisable value concept

B Prudence concept

C Realisation concept

D Going concern concept

171 What is the purpose of charging depreciation in the accounts of a business?

A To ensure that funds are available for the eventual replacement of the asset.

B To reduce the cost of the asset in the statement of financial position to its estimated market value.

C To allocate the cost of the non-current asset over the accounting periods expected to benefit from its use.

D To comply with the prudence concept.

172 An entity has an asset which cost $100,000. It is expected to last for ten years and have a scrap value of $10,000. The entity is going to depreciate this asset at 20% using the reducing balance method.

What will the depreciation charge on this asset be in its second year?

A $14,400

B $16,000

C $18,000

D $20,000

173 Which TWO of the following are reasons for maintaining a non-current asset register?

	Selected answer
To calculate the total balance outstanding on loans raised to purchase non-current assets	
To help in carrying out the physical verification of non-current assets	
To calculate the profit or loss on disposal of non-current assets	
To eliminate the need to maintain ledger accounts relating to non-current assets	

174 Baz is recording the invoice for the purchase of a new plant and equipment.

Which TWO of the following items should be capitalised as part of the cost of the asset?

	Selected answer
Cost of staff training to use the new plant and equipment	
Installation costs	
Three-year maintenance agreement	
Delivery costs	

175 The opening balance on Derv's motor vehicles at cost account was $140,000. The opening balance on depreciation of motor vehicles was $60,000. The business purchased new vehicles costing $30,000 during the year. No vehicles were sold. The business depreciates vehicles at 25% on the reducing balance basis, with a full year's depreciation in the year of acquisition and none in the year of disposal.

What is the closing balance on Derv 's depreciation of motor vehicles account?

$

176 Which of the following provides a definition of a non-current asset register?

A It is an alternative name for the non-current asset ledger account.

B It is a list of the physical non-current assets rather than their financial cost.

C It is a schedule of planned maintenance of non-current assets for use by the plant engineer.

D It is a schedule of the cost and other information about each individual non-current asset.

177 An entity's non-current asset register shows a carrying amount of $125,600. The non-current asset account in the general ledger shows a carrying amount of $135,600.

What would explain the difference if it is due to a disposed asset NOT having been deducted from the non-current assets ledger?

A There were disposal proceeds of $15,000 and a profit on disposal of $5,000

B There were disposal proceeds of $15,000 and a carrying amount of $5,000

C There were disposal proceeds of $15,000 and a loss on disposal of $5,000

D There were disposal proceeds of $5,000 and a carrying amount of $5,000

The following information relates to questions 178 and 179.

Tao bought a machine for use in the business on 1 November 20X4. Tao gave the supplier a cheque for $11,570 and traded in an old machine. The supplier allowed Tao $4,430 in part exchange for the old machine. Tao depreciates machinery using the reducing balance basis at the rate of 20% per annum. The old machine had cost $12,000 and had been depreciated by $5,856.

Note: in the exam, all questions will be independent, and not based on a common scenario.

178 What was the profit or loss on the trade in of the old machine?

A A profit of $1,426

B A profit of $1,714

C A loss of $1,426

D A loss of $1,714

179 What was the depreciation charge on the new machine for the year to 31 October 20X5?

$

180 Information relating to two non-current assets was as follows:

	Cost	Accumulated depreciation at 1 January 20X4	Depreciation charge for 20X4
	$	$	$
Asset 1	100,000	50,000	7,500
Asset 2	50,000	10,000	7,500

Which depreciation method has been applied to each asset?

	15% straight-line	15% reducing balance
Asset 1		
Asset 2		

181 When Mitch purchased a new car, an old car was traded-in as part exchange. Mitch made the correct entry for the part-exchange value of $3,500 in the non-current asset disposal account.

What other entry is needed to complete the double entry for the part-exchange value of $3,500?

A A debit entry in the motor vehicles at cost account

B A credit entry in the motor vehicles at cost account

C A debit entry in the bank account

D A credit entry in the bank account

182 On 1 July 20X4 Yan bought a machine for $15,500. Yan depreciates machinery at the rate of 20% per annum using the reducing balance basis. A full year's depreciation is charged in the year an asset is purchased. Yan's year end is 31 October.

What was the depreciation charge on the machine for the year to 31 October 20X6?

$

183 **Which of the following would normally be recorded in a non-current asset register?**

(i) the location of each asset

(ii) the serial number of each asset

(iii) accumulated depreciation on each asset

A (i) only

B (ii) and (iii) only

C (i) and (iii) only

D (i), (ii) and (iii)

184 Quiang's year end is 30 September. Quiang depreciates office furniture at 15% per annum using the straight line basis. A full year's depreciation is charged in the year an asset is purchased, and no depreciation is charged in the year it is sold. In March 20X5 Quiang bought office furniture for $80,000.

If Quiang sells the office furniture for $39,000 in July 20X8, what will be the profit or loss on disposal?

A A profit of $7,000

B A loss of $7,000

C A profit of $5,000

D A loss of $5,000

185 On 1 January 20X7, an entity purchased an item of plant. The invoice showed:

	$
Cost of plant	48,000
Delivery to factory	400
One year warranty covering breakdown	800
	49,200

In addition, modifications to the factory building costing $2,200 were necessary to enable the plant to be installed.

What amount should be capitalised for the plant in the accounting records of the business?

$

186 A non-current asset was purchased at the beginning of Year 1 for $2,400 and depreciated by 20% per annum using the reducing balance method. At the beginning of Year 4 it was sold for $1,200.

What was the profit or loss on disposal?

A A loss on disposal of $240.00

B A loss on disposal of $28.80

C A profit on disposal of $28.80

D A profit on disposal of $240.00

187 An entity's non-current assets had a carrying amount of $125,000. An asset which had cost $12,000 was sold for $9,000, at a profit of $2,000.

What was the revised carrying amount of non-current assets?

$

188 A non-current asset was disposed of for $2,200 during the last accounting year. It had been purchased exactly three years earlier for $5,000, with an expected residual value of $500, and had been depreciated on the reducing balance basis, at 20% per annum.

What was the loss on disposal?

$

189 Which TWO of the following items should be accounted for as asset expenditure?

	Selected answer
The purchase of a car for a member of the sales department to visit clients	
The purchase of a car for resale by a car dealer	
Legal fees incurred on the purchase of a building	
The cost of painting a building	

190 A car was purchased for $12,000 on 1 April 20X1 and has been depreciated at 20% each year straight line, assuming no residual value. The accounting policy of the business is to charge a full year's depreciation in the year of purchase and no depreciation in the year of sale. The car was traded in for a replacement vehicle on 1 August 20X4 for an agreed figure of $5,000.

What was the profit on the disposal of the vehicle for the year ended 31 December 20X4?

$

191 A business accounted for the repair of an item of plant and machinery as asset expenditure in the accounting records.

What is the effect of this error upon the profit for the year and also upon the carrying amount of assets included in the statement of financial position before the error is corrected?

A Profit for the year is understated and assets on the statement of financial position are overstated.

B Profit for the year is overstated and assets on the statement of financial position are overstated.

C Profit for the year is understated and assets on the statement of financial position are understated.

D Profit for the year is overstated and assets on the statement of financial position are understated.

192 A business accounted for the purchase of a new delivery truck as a motor expense in the accounting records.

What is the effect of this error upon the profit for the year and also upon the carrying amount of assets included in the statement of financial position before the error is corrected?

A Profit for the year is understated and assets on the statement of financial position are overstated.

B Profit for the year is overstated and assets on the statement of financial position are overstated.

C Profit for the year is understated and assets on the statement of financial position are understated.

D Profit for the year is overstated and assets on the statement of financial position are understated.

193 Smart Co purchased an item of plant at a cost of $100,000 in 1 January 20X2. It was expected to last for ten years and have a scrap value of $10,000. Smart Co depreciates non-current assets at 20% on the reducing balance basis. The item of plant was sold on 1 April 20X4 for sale proceeds of $70,000. It is Smart Co's policy to charge a full year of depreciation in the year of purchase and none in the year of disposal. Smart Co has an accounting year end of 31 December.

What was the profit on disposal on this asset?

$

194 Marty purchased an item of plant at a cost of $100,000 in 1 January 20X2. It was expected to last for six years and had an estimated scrap value of $10,000 at the end of that time. Marty depreciates non-current assets on a straight-line basis, with a proportionate charge in the year of purchase and disposal. Marty has an accounting year end of 31 December. The item of plant subsequently was sold on 1 April 20X4 for sale proceeds of $60,000.

What was the loss on disposal on this asset?

$

The following information relates to questions 195 to 199

A machine which had cost of $20,000 and had accumulated depreciation of $17,200 was sold during 20X7 for $4,800. The total cost of machinery shown in the December 20X6 statement of financial position was $180,000 and the related accumulated depreciation was $92,000. The business uses 10% straight-line depreciation on machinery and no depreciation is charged in the year in which an asset is sold.

Note: in the exam, all questions will be independent, and not based on a common scenario.

---

195 **What was the balance on the accumulated depreciation account at 31 December 20X7?**

$

196 **What was the profit on disposal of the machine?**

$

197 **What was the annual depreciation charge for 20X7?**

$

198 What entries are required in the disposal of asset account in the general ledger to record the sale of the machine in 20X7?

	Debit	**Credit**
A	Accumulated depreciation $9,600	Bank $4,800 Machinery $4,800
B	Machinery $3,400 Accumulated depreciation $1,400	Bank $4,800
C	Machinery $22,000	Bank $4,800 Accumulated depreciation $17,200
D	Machinery $20,000 Profit on disposal $2,000	Accumulated depreciation $17,200 Bank $4,800

199 Which of the following best describes the gain or loss on the disposal of a non-current?

A The amount by which management over or under charged depreciation for the asset.

B The extent to which the asset's underlying value changed during its useful life.

C The correction of forecasting errors when the asset's useful life and residual values were estimated.

D The remaining value after depreciation has been taken into account.

200 At 30 September 20X2, the following balances existed in the records of Lambda Co:

Plant and equipment:

Cost	$860,000
Accumulated depreciation	$397,000

During the year ended 30 September 20X3, plant with a written down value of $37,000 was sold for $49,000. The plant had originally cost $80,000. Plant purchased during the year cost $180,000. The accounting policy of the business is to charge a full year's depreciation in the year of acquisition of an asset and none in the year of sale, using a rate of 10% on the straight line basis.

What carrying amount should appear in Lambda Co's statement of financial position at 30 September 20X3 for plant and equipment?

$ ______

201 A business with an accounting year end of 31 October purchased a non-current asset on 1 July 20X3 for $126,000.

Depreciation is charged at the rate of 15% per annum using the reducing balance basis. On 30 September 20X7 the asset was sold for $54,800. It is the policy of the business to charge a proportionate amount of depreciation in both the year of acquisition and the year of disposal.

What was the loss on sale of the asset (to the nearest $)?

A $19,792

B $8,603

C $7,674

D $1,106

202 A car was purchased by a business in May 20X1 as follows:

	$
Cost	10,000
Road tax	150
Total	10,150

The business has an accounting year end 31 December. The car was traded in for a replacement vehicle in August 20X5 at an agreed value of $5,000.

It was depreciated at 25% per annum using the reducing-balance method, charging a full year's depreciation in the year of purchase and none in the year of sale.

What was the profit on disposal of the vehicle during the year ended December 20X5?

$

203 A business had non-current assets with a carrying amount of $200,000 at 1 August 20X2. During the year ended 31 July 20X3, the business sold non-current assets for $25,000 on which it made a loss of $5,000. The depreciation charge for the year was $20,000.

What was the carrying amount of non-current assets at 31 July 20X3?

$

204 A non-current asset costing $12,500 was sold at a loss of $4,500. Depreciation had been provided using the reducing balance method, at 20% per annum since its purchase.

Which of the following correctly describes the sale proceeds and length of time for which the asset had been owned?

	Sale proceeds	Length of ownership
A	Cannot be calculated	Cannot be calculated
B	Cannot be calculated	Two years
C	$8,000	Cannot be calculated
D	$8,000	Two years

205 A machine cost $9,000. It has an expected useful life of 6 years, and an expected residual value of $1,000. It is to be depreciated at 30% per annum using the reducing balance basis.

A full year's depreciation is charged in the year of purchase, with none in the year of sale. During year 4, it is sold for $3,000.

What was the loss on disposal of the machine?

$

206 Dion sold a machine for $5,300. The machine had been bought three years previously at a cost of $10,000. At the date of sale accumulated depreciation charges amounted to $4,800.

What was the profit on disposal of the machine?

$

207 Jaime sold a machine which originally cost $14,900. At the date of sale, the accumulated depreciation on the machine was $8,940. The sale proceeds were $7,455.

What was the profit or loss on the sale of the machine?

A A profit of $1,485

B A loss of $1,485

C A loss of $1,495

D A profit of $1,495

208 **Which of the following should be accounted for as asset expenditure?**

A The purchase of a car by a car dealer for re-sale

B The purchase of a delivery van by a business

C The cost of repairing a delivery van by a business

D The cost of vehicle insurance by a business

209 A machine was purchased for $18,000 on 1 April 20X1 and has been depreciated at 20% each year on the straight line basis, assuming no residual value. The depreciation policy of the business is to charge a full year's depreciation in the year of purchase and no depreciation in the year of sale. The car was traded in for a replacement vehicle on 1 August 20X4 for an agreed figure of $8,000.

What was the profit or loss on the disposal of the vehicle for the year ended 31 December 20X4?

A Profit $800

B Profit $2,800

C Profit $4,400

D Profit $7,200

210 Information relating to two asset disposal transactions was as follows:

	Cost	Accumulated Depreciation	Disposal proceeds
	$	$	$
Asset 1	15,000	8,500	7,500
Asset 2	17,000	9,500	6,500

For each disposal transaction, was there a profit or loss on disposal?

	Profit on disposal	Loss on disposal
Asset 1		
Asset 2		

ACCRUALS AND PREPAYMENTS

211 Troy, a property business, received receipts directly into the bank from tenants totalling $838,600 during the year ended 31 December 20X6.

Figures for rent in advance and in arrears at the beginning and end of the year were:

	31 December 20X5	31 December 20X6
	$	$
Rent received in advance	102,600	88,700
Rent in arrears (all subsequently received)	42,300	48,400

What amount should be included in Troy's statement of profit or loss for the year ended 31 December 20X6 for rental income?

$

212 Details of Bartlett's insurance policy are shown below:

Premium for year ended 31 March 20X6 paid April 20X5 $10,800

Premium for year ending 31 March 20X7 paid April 20X6 $12,000

What figures should be included in the Bartlett's financial statements for the year ended 30 June 20X6?

	Statement of profit or loss	Statement of financial position
	$	$
A	11,100	9,000 prepayment
B	11,700	9,000 prepayment
C	11,100	9,000 accrual
D	11,700	9,000 accrual

213 Vine Co sublets part of its office accommodation. The rent is received quarterly in advance on 1 January, 1 April, 1 July and 1 October. The annual rent has been $24,000 for some years, but it was increased to $30,000 from 1 July 20X5.

What amounts for rent should appear in Vine Co's financial statements for the year ended 31 January 20X6?

	Statement of profit or loss	Statement of financial position
	$	$
A	27,500	5,000 accrued income
B	27,000	2,500 accrued income
C	27,000	2,500 prepaid income
D	27,500	5,000 prepaid income

214 On 1 September, the motor expenses account showed 4 months' insurance prepaid of $80 and petrol accrued of $95. During September, the outstanding petrol invoice was paid, plus further invoices of $245. At 30 September there is a further outstanding petrol invoice of $120.

What amount should be shown in the statement of profit or loss for motor expenses for the month of September?

$

215 On 1 May 20X0, Fran paid a rent bill of $1,800 for the period to 30 April 20X1.

What is the charge to the statement of profit or loss and the entry in the statement of financial position for the year ended 30 November 20X0?

A $1,050 charge to statement of profit or loss and prepayment of $750 in the statement of financial position.

B $1,050 charge to statement of profit or loss and accrual of $750 in the statement of financial position.

C $1,800 charge to statement of profit or loss and no entry in the statement of financial position.

D $750 charge to statement of profit or loss and prepayment of $1,050 in the statement of financial position.

216 The electricity account for the year ended 30 June 20X3 was as follows:

	$
Opening balance for electricity accrued at 1 July 20X2	300
Bank payments made during the year:	
1 August 20X2 for three months to 31 July 20X2	600
1 November 20X2 for three months to 31 October 20X2	720
1 February 20X3 for three months to 31 January 20X3	900
30 June 20X3 for three months to 30 April 20X3	840

Which of the following are the appropriate amounts to include in the financial statements for electricity charges?

	Accrued at June 20X3	Charged to statement of profit or loss, year ended 30 June 20X3
A	$Nil	$3,060
B	$460	$3,320
C	$560	$3,320
D	$560	$3,420

217 Farthing Co's year-end is 30 September. On 1 January 20X6 the entity took out a loan of $100,000 with annual interest payable of 12%. The interest is payable in equal instalments on the first day of April, July, October and January in arrears.

How much should be charged to the statement of profit or loss account for the year ended 30 September 20X6, and how much should be accrued on the statement of financial position?

	Statement of profit or loss	Statement of financial position
A	$12,000	$3,000
B	$9,000	$3,000
C	$9,000	Nil
D	$6,000	$3,000

218 On the 1 January 20X8, a business had prepaid insurance of $10,000. On 1 August 20X8, it paid, in full, the annual insurance invoice of $36,000, to cover the following year.

What is the amount charged in the statement of profit or loss and the amount shown in the statement of financial position at 31 December 20X8?

	Statement of profit or loss	Statement of financial position
	$	$
A	5,000	24,000
B	22,000	23,000
C	25,000	21,000
D	36,000	15,000

219 Which one of the following statements is correct?

A Accruals decrease profit

B Accrued income decreases profit

C A prepayment is a liability

D An accrual is an asset

220 Fran's year-end is 31 March. On 1 January 20X3 Fran took out a loan of $250,000 with annual interest of 10%. The interest is payable in equal instalments on the first day of April, July, October and January in arrears.

How much should be charged to the statement of profit or loss account for the year ended 31 March 20X3, and how much should be accrued on the statement of financial position?

	Statement of profit or loss	Statement of financial position
A	$25,000	$18,750
B	$6,250	$6,250
C	$6,250	Nil
D	$18,750	6,250

221 On 23 May 20X7, Jools used cash to pay the rent in advance on the business premises for the three months to 31 August 20X7.

On 23 May, how is Jools' accounting equation affected by this transaction?

	Assets	Liabilities	Capital
A	Unchanged	Unchanged	Unchanged
B	Unchanged	Reduced	Reduced
C	Reduced	Unchanged	Unchanged
D	Reduced	Unchanged	Reduced

222 In September 20X6 Ali paid $7,800 for rent for the four months from 1 October 20X6.

What should be reported on Ali's statement of financial position at 30 November 20X6?

A An accrual of $3,900

B An accrual of $1,950

C A prepayment of $3,900

D A prepayment of $1,950

223 In the year to 30 November 20X6 Nimat paid $1,765 for electricity. At 1 December 20X5 Nimat had an accrual of $264 for electricity. At 30 November 20X6 the accrual was $312.

What is the charge for electricity in Nimat's statement of profit or loss for the year ended 30 November 20X6?

$

224 When the general ledger accounts of Lei were closed off at 30 April 20X7 Lei's wages expense account had a debit balance of $87,963. Lei also had to make an accrual of $1,268 for outstanding wages.

What is Lei's opening credit balance for wages at 1 May 20X7?

$

225 The rent account for a business was as follows:

Rent

		$			$
1/1/X5	Bal b/d	1,000			
1/2/X5	Bank	3,000			
1/5/X5	Bank	3,000			
1/8/X5	Bank	3,600	31/12/X5	Profit or loss	13,000
1/11/X5	Bank	3,600	31/12/X5	Bal c/d	1,200
		14,200			14,200
1/1/X6	Bal b/d	1,200			

Which of the following best describes the rent expense?

A Cash paid $13,000 and Charge for year $13,200

B Cash paid $13,000 and Charge for year $13,000

C Cash paid $13,200 and Charge for year $13,000

D Cash paid $13,200 and Charge for year $13,200

226 A business compiling its accounts for the year to 31 January each year, pays rent quarterly in advance on 1 January, 1 April, 1 July and 1 October each year. After remaining unchanged for some years, the rent was increased from $24,000 per year to $30,000 per year as from 1 July 20X3.

What is the rent expense that should appear in the statement of profit or loss for the year ended 31 January 20X4?

A $30,000

B $27,000

C $27,500

D $24,000

227 On 1 May 20X3, Blister Co paid a rent bill of $1,800 for the period to 30 April 20X4. What is the charge to the statement of profit or loss and the entry in the statement of financial position for the year ended 30 November 20X3?

A $1,050 charge to profit or loss and prepayment of $750 in the statement of financial position

B $1,050 charge to profit or loss and accrual of $750 in the statement of financial position

C $1,800 charge to profit or loss and no entry in the statement of financial position

D $750 charge to profit or loss and prepayment of $1,050 in the statement of financial position

228 On 1 June 20X2, H Co paid an insurance invoice of $2,400 for the year to 31 May 20X3. What is the charge to the statement of profit or loss and the entry in the statement of financial position for the year ended 31 December 20X2?

A $1,000 profit or loss and prepayment of $1,400

B $1,400 profit or loss and accrual of $1,000

C $1,400 profit or loss and prepayment of $1,000

D $2,400 profit or loss and no entry in the statement of financial position

229 At 31 March 20X3, accrued rent payable was $300. During the year ended 31 March 20X4, rent paid was $4,000, including an invoice for $1,200 for the quarter ended 30 April 20X4.

What was the charge to profit or loss for rent payable for the year ended 31 March 20X4?

$ ________

230 The electricity account of an entity for the year ended 30 June 20X3 was as follows:

	$
Opening balance for electricity accrued at 1 July 20X2	300
Payments made during the year:	
1 August 20X2 for three months to 31 July 20X2	600
1 November 20X2 for three months to 31 October 20X2	720
1 February 20X3 for three months to 31 January 20X3	900
30 June 20X3 for three months to 30 April 20X3	840

Which of the following are the appropriate entries for electricity?

	Accrued at 30 June 20X3	**Charged to profit or loss year ended 30 June 20X3**
A	$Nil	$3,060
B	$460	$3,320
C	$560	$3,320
D	$560	$3,420

231 The annual insurance premium for S Co for the period 1 July 20X3 to 30 June 20X4 was $13,200, which was 10% more than the previous year. Insurance premiums are paid on 1 July.

What was the profit or loss charge for insurance for the year ended 31 December 20X3?

$

232 Arlo paid $5,520 for rent for the six-month period to 31 August 20X1.

What prepayment is required when preparing accounts for the year ended 30 June 20X1?

$

233 The last electricity bill received by Grax was for the three-month period to 30 September 20X1. This bill was for $2,100.

What accrual is required when preparing the accounts for the year to 30 November 20X1?

$

234 Jax is preparing the year-end accounts and has to deal with a prepayment for rent.

Which of the following statements is correct?

A The prepayment will increase the charge to profit or loss

B The prepayment will reduce the charge to profit or loss

C The prepayment has no effect on profit or loss

D The prepayment will only affect profit or loss

235 When the draft accounts were prepared, Shen included $1,400 as an accrual for rent for two months. However, Shen should have provided for only one month's rent.

How will Shen's current liabilities be affected when the accrual is adjusted?

A Reduced by $1,400

B Increased by $1,400

C Reduced by $700

D Increased by $700

236 Kelan's draft accounts for the year to 31 October 20X5 report a loss of $1,486. When Kelan prepared the accounts, an accrual of $1,625 and a prepayment of $834 were omitted in error.

What is Kelan's profit or loss for the year to 31 October 20X5 following the inclusion of the accrual and prepayment?

A A loss of $695

B A loss of $2,277

C A loss of $3,945

D A profit of $1,807

237 Dai is preparing final accounts for the year to 30 April 20X6. The last payment Dai made for electricity was in March 20X6 when a payment of $3,270 was made for the three months to 28 February 20X6.

What adjustment does Dai need to make when preparing the final accounts for the year to 30 April 20X6?

A A prepayment of $1,090

B An accrual of $1,090

C A prepayment of $2,180

D An accrual of $2,180

238 In Theo's statement of profit or loss for the year ended 31 May 20X6 the charge for motor repairs was $2,850. This included an accrual of $220.

When Theo's opening trial balance at 1 June 20X6 is prepared, what is the correct balance on the motor repairs account?

A $220 (debit)

B $220 (credit)

C $2,850 (debit)

D $2,850 (credit)

239 Information relating to two expenses was as follows:

	Opening accrual	**Cash paid**	**P&L expense**
	$	$	$
Repairs and renewals	2,000	39,500	36,500
Light and heat	1,000	25,000	25,500

For each transaction, was there an accrual or prepayment at the end of the accounting period?

	Accrual	**Prepayment**
Repairs and renewals		
Light and heat		

RECEIVABLES, PAYABLES AND PROVISIONS

240 Newell Co's receivables' account shows a balance at the end of the year of $58,200 before making the following adjustments:

(i) Newell Co wishes to write off debts amounting to $8,900 as they are regarded as irrecoverable.

(ii) Newell Co also wishes to make an allowance for two receivables of $1,350 and $750 respectively.

Newell Co's allowance for receivables at the end of the previous year was $5,650.

What is the total charge to the statement of profit or loss in respect of the above?

$

241 In the statement of financial position at 31 December 20X5, Guang reported net receivables of $12,000. During 20X6 Guang made sales on credit of $125,000 and receipts from credit customers amounting to $115,500. At 31 December 20X6, Guang wished to write off debts of $7,100 and increase the allowance for receivables by $950 to $2,100.

What is the net receivables figure to include in the statement of financial position at 31 December 20X6?

$

242 At 1 July 20X5, Yanlin's allowance for receivables was $48,000. At 30 June 20X6, trade receivables amounted to $838,000. It was decided to write off $72,000 of these debts and adjust the allowance for receivables to $60,000.

What are the final amounts for inclusion in Yanlin's statement of financial position at 30 June 20X6?

	Trade receivables	**Allowance for receivables**	**Net balance**
	$	$	$
A	838,000	60,000	778,000
B	766,000	60,000	706,000
C	766,000	108,000	658,000
D	838,000	108,000	730,000

243 During the year ended 30 September 20X8, Fauntleroy Co had sales of $7,000,000. Year-end receivables amounted to 5% of annual sales. At 1 October 20X7, the allowance for receivables was $11,667 and this should be increased to $14,000 at 30 September 20X8.

During the year ended 30 September 20X8, irrecoverable debts amounting to $3,200 were written off and debts amounting to $450 which had been written off previously were recovered.

What is the irrecoverable debt expense for the year?

$

244 Following a mid-year review of its aged receivables' listing, Pluto Co identified three irrecoverable debts totalling $630 which should be written off. One of the debts, for $150, was already included in the allowance for receivables.

What accounting entries should Pluto Co make to write off the irrecoverable debts?

	Debit	**Credit**
A	Irrecoverable debts $480	Trade receivables $480
B	Irrecoverable debts $630	Trade receivables $630
C	Irrecoverable debts $480 Allowance for receivables $150	Trade receivables $630
D	Irrecoverable debts $630	Trade receivables $480 Allowance for receivables $150

245 At its accounting year end of 30 November 20X6, Venus Co decided to write off irrecoverable debts of $425 and also to increase the allowance for receivables by $160.

What accounting entries should Venus Co make to update the general ledger to reflect these circumstances?

	Debit	**Credit**
A	Trade receivables $585	Irrecoverable debts $425 Allowance for receivables $160
B	Irrecoverable debts $425 Allowance for receivables $160	Trade receivables $585
C	Irrecoverable debts $585	Trade receivables $425 Allowance for receivables $160
D	Irrecoverable debts $585	Allowance for receivables $585

246 At its accounting year end of 31 October 20X3, Neptune Co decided to write off irrecoverable debts of $673 and also to reduce the allowance for receivables by $184.

What accounting entries should Neptune Co make to update the general ledger to reflect these circumstances?

	Debit	**Credit**
A	Trade receivables $673	Irrecoverable debts $489 Allowance for receivables $184
B	Irrecoverable debts $184 Allowance for receivables $489	Trade receivables $673
C	Irrecoverable debts $857	Trade receivables $673 Allowance for receivables $160
D	Irrecoverable debts $489 Allowance for receivables $184	Receivables $673

247 During its accounting year end to 31 May 20X7, Jupiter Co unexpectedly received a receipt of $382 in relation to a debt which had been written off earlier during the year.

What accounting entries should Jupiter Co make to update the general ledger to reflect this situation?

	Debit	Credit
A	Bank $382	Sundry income $382
B	Bank $382	Receivables $382
C	Bank $382	Allowance for receivables $382
D	Bank $382	Irrecoverable debts $382

248 During its accounting year end to 30 April 20X1, Earth Co agreed with Trader Co, who it both purchased goods from, and sold goods to, on credit terms, to contra an amount of $1,500 off the balances due to each other.

What accounting entries should Earth Co make in its general ledger to record this situation?

	Debit	Credit
A	Trade receivables $1,500	Trade payables $1,500
B	Trade payables $1,500	Trade receivables $1,500
C	Sales $1,500	Purchases $1,500
D	Purchases $1,500	Sales $1,500

249 During its accounting year end to 29 February 20X5, Saturn Co agreed with Acme Co, who it both purchased goods from, and sold goods to, on credit terms, to contra the maximum possible amount of the balances due to each other. At the date of this agreement, Saturn Co had a receivables ledger account balance for Acme Co of $685 and a payable ledger account balance of $565.

What accounting entries should Saturn Co make in its general ledger to record this situation?

	Debit	Credit
A	Trade payables $685	Trade receivables $685
B	Trade payables $565	Trade receivables $565
C	Trade receivables $565	Trade payables $565
D	Trade receivables $685	Trade payables $685

250 During its accounting year end to 29 February 20X5, Neptune Co agreed with Sun Co, who it both purchased goods from, and sold goods to, on credit terms, to contra an amount that left the a balance outstanding from Sun Co due to Neptune Co of $750. At the date of this this agreement, Neptune Co had a receivables ledger account balance for Sun Co of $2,685 and a payable ledger account balance of $2,565.

What accounting entries should Neptune Co make in its general ledger to record this situation?

	Debit	**Credit**
A	Trade payables $1,935	Trade receivables $1,935
B	Trade receivables $1,815	Trade payables $1,815
C	Trade receivables $1,935	Trade payables $1,935
D	Trade payables $1,815	Trade receivables $1,815

251 At 1 August 20X4, Wallaby's trade receivables were $43,750 and the allowance for receivables was $1,875. At 31 July 20X5, trade receivables amounted to $42,300. It was decided to write off $3,700 of these debts and adjust the allowance for receivables to $2,250.

What are the final balances included in Wallaby's financial statements for the year ended 31 July 20X5?

	Trade receivables	**Allowance for receivables**	**Irrecoverable debts**
	$	$	$
A	38,600	4,075	2,250
B	40,050	2,250	4,075
C	38,600	2,250	4,075
D	38,975	2,250	3,700

252 On 1 January 20X3 Tipton Co's trade receivables were $10,000. The following information relates to the year ended 31 December 20X3:

	$
Credit sales	100,000
Banked receipts	90,000
Irrecoverable debts written off in year	800
Discounts received	700

Cash receipts include $1,000 in respect of a receivable previously written off.

What was the carrying amount of receivables at 31 December 20X3?

$

253 A business has been notified that a customer who owed $500 has been declared insolvent. The business had previously made an allowance against this receivable.

What accounting entries are required to account for the amount due from the insolvent customer?

	Debit	Credit
A	Irrecoverable debts account	Receivables' ledger account
B	Receivables' ledger account	Irrecoverable debts account
C	Allowance for receivables account	Receivables' ledger account
D	Receivables' ledger account	Allowance for receivables account

254 Headington was owed $37,500 by its customers at 1 January 20X8 and $49,000 at 31 December 20X8.

During 20X8, cash sales of $263,500 and credit sales of $357,500 were made, contras with payables amounted to $1,750 and discounts received totalled $21,400. Irrecoverable debts of $3,500 were written off and Headington wishes to increase its allowance for receivables from $7,500 to $10,000.

What was the cash received from receivables during the year ended 31 December 20X8?

$

255 Alex had total receivables of $87,000 and an allowance for receivables of $2,500 at the start of the accounting year.

During the year, two specific debts were written off, one for $800 and the other for $550. A debt of $350 that had been written off as irrecoverable in the previous year was paid during the year. At the year-end, total receivables were $90,000 and the allowance for receivables was $2,300.

What was the charge to the statement of profit or loss for the year in relating to irrecoverable debts and the change in the allowance for receivables?

$

256 **What is the effect of an increase in the allowance for receivables?**

A It will result in an increase in net current assets

B It will result in a decrease in net current assets

C It will result in an increase in sales

D It will result in a decrease in drawings

257 At 31 December 20X7, Chester's receivables' balance was $230,000. Chester wishes to make a specific allowance for Em's debt of $450, Lu's debt of $980 and Sandy's debt of $5,000.

What amount should be credited to the statement of profit or loss relating to the allowance for receivables if the allowance at 1 January 20X7 was $11,700?

$

258 At 31 March 20X9 Shi was owed $47,744 by customers. At the same date, Shi's allowance for receivables was $3,500.

How should these balances be reported on Shi's statement of financial position at 31 March 20X9?

A $44,244 as a current asset

B $3,500 as a current asset and $47,744 as a current liability

C $47,744 as a current asset and $3,500 as a current liability

D $51,244 as a current asset

259 The allowance for receivables in the ledger of Baz at 31 October 20X1 was $9,000. During the year ended 31 October 20X2, irrecoverable debts of $5,000 were written off.

Accounts receivable balances at 31 October 20X2 were $120,000 and, based upon a review of receivables at that date, the allowance for receivables required was $6,000.

What was the total charge for irrecoverable and debts and change in allowance for receivables in the statement of profit or loss for the year ended 31 October 20X2?

$

260 At 1 November 20X4 Joginder's receivables allowance was $5,670. At 31 October 20X5 Joginder was owed $275,600 by customers. Following a review of receivables, Joginder has determined that an allowance of $5,512 is required at 31 October 20X5.

What amount should be credited in Joginder's statement of profit or loss for the year ended 31 October 20X5 relating to the change in the allowance for receivables?

$

261 Which of the following is the correct definition of a provision?

A A provision is an amount that may need to be paid by a business

B A provision is a liability of uncertain timing or amount

C A provision is a specific amount that will be paid on a specified date

D A provision is an amount that may not need to be paid by a business

262 What is the difference between a liability and a provision?

A A provision can relate only to items due after more than one year, whereas a liability may be classified as due within, or after one year

B A provision is a confirmed obligation, whereas la liability is an obligation of uncertain timing or amount

C A provision can only relate to items due within one year, whereas a liability may be classified as due within, or after, one year

D A provision is an obligation of uncertain timing and/or amount, whereas a liability is a confirmed obligation

263 In which of the following situations would a car repairer be required to recognise a provision in its financial statements?

A A customer suffered scalding injury when drinking a hot drink provided by the car repairer whilst also trying to work on their laptop and also trying to read a document

B A customer suffered an injury whilst in the customer reception area and standing on a chair trying to see into the repair workshop area

C A customer slipped on grease on the repair workshop floor when discussing a car repair with a member of staff and suffered a broken leg as a consequence

D A customer suffered an injury when driving away too quickly, having collected the car from the care repair workshop

264 Koala Co has a bank loan of $30,000, on which a variable rate of interest is paid quarterly, which is due for repayment on 31 December 20X6. At the accounting year end of 30 November 20X3, interest on the loan outstanding was estimated to be $1,000.

Which of the following statements best explains the situation at 30 November 20X3?

A Koala has a current liability of $1,000 and a provision of $30,000 for repayment of the loan.

B Koala has a non-current liability of $30,000 and should recognise an accrual for $1,000

C Koala Co has a non-current liability of $30,000 and a current liability of $1,000

D Koala Co has a non-current liability of $31,000

265 Ping commenced trading on 1 January 20X5 selling microwave ovens at a price of $300 each. Ping allows customers one month from the date of sale to return goods if they are unsatisfactory for any reason and customers will be given a full refund. During the first year of trading to 31 December 20X5, Ping sold 150 microwave ovens each month and, on average, five microwave ovens are returned in the month following sale. Customer refunds are made in the same month as the microwave is returned.

What provision should be included in Ping's financial statements for the year ended 31 December 20X5?

$

266 Kai allows customers to return faulty goods within 10 days of purchase. At 31 October 20X4 Kai had a provision of $6,548 for sales returns. At 31 October 20X5 Kai calculated that the provision required should be $4,940.

What should be reported in Kai's statement of profit or loss for the year to 31 October 20X5 in relation to this provision?

A A charge of $4,940

B A credit of $4,940

C A credit of $1,608

D A charge of $1,608

267 Luca is a second-hand motorcycle dealer. If a motorcycle develops a fault within 60 days of the sale, Luca will repair it under warranty free of charge. At 30 September 20X5 Luca had made a provision for warranty repairs of $5,500. At 30 September 20X6, Luca estimated that the provision required for warranty repairs should be $6,300.

What accounting entries should be made by Luca to account for the increase in the provision required at 30 September 20X6?

A	Debit Warranty repairs $800, and	Credit Provision $800
B	Debit Warranty repairs $6,300, and	Credit Provision $6,300
C	Debit Provision $800, and	Credit Warranty repairs $800
D	Debit Provision $6,300, and	Credit Warranty repairs $6,300

268 Chun allows customers to return faulty goods within 14 days of purchase. At 30 November 20X5 Chun made a provision of $6,548 for sales returns. At 30 November 20X6 Chun calculated that the provision should be $7,634.

What should be reported in Chun's statement of profit or loss for the year to 30 November 20X6 in relation to this provision?

A A charge of $7,634

B A credit of $7,634

C A charge of $1,086

D A credit of $1,086

269 Niral is a second-hand car dealer. If a car develops a fault within 30 days of the sale, Niral will repair it free of charge. At 30 April 20X4 Niral had made a provision for repairs of $2,500. At 30 April 20X5 Niral calculated that the provision should be $2,000.

What entry should be made for the provision in Niral's statement of profit or loss for the year to 30 April 20X5?

A A charge of $500

B A credit of $500

C A charge of $2,000

D A credit of $2,000

CAPITAL AND FINANCE COSTS

270 Armani started a business and paid $15,000 into the business bank account. Armani also obtained a bank loan of $5,000 to help finance the business.

How should these two transactions be classified in the statement of financial position?

A Proprietor's capital of $20,000

B Business liabilities of $20,000

C Proprietor's capital of $5,000 and a business liability of $15,000

D Proprietor's capital of $15,000 and a business liability of $5,000

271 A sole trader had opening capital of $12,000 and closing capital of $14,500. During the period, the owner introduced capital of $1,500 and withdrew $6,000 for own use.

What was the profit for the period?

$

272 A sole trader had opening capital of $12,000 and closing capital of $14,500. During the period, the owner made a loss of $13,000 and withdrew $7,500 for own use.

What was capital introduced into the business during the year?

$

273 Lalan, a sole trader, had an opening capital balance of $23,000. During the accounting year, Lalan made a loss of $2,500. In addition, Lalan introduced capital of 3,000 and made drawings of $8,200.

What was Lalan's capital account balance at the end of the accounting period?

$

274 Manvi, a sole trader, had an opening capital balance of $35,000. During the accounting year, Manvi made drawings of $14,600. At the end of the accounting year, Manvi's capital account balance was $30,000.

What was Manvi's profit for the year?

$

275 Ronnie, a sole trader, had a closing capital balance of $42,500. During the accounting year, Ronnie made drawings of $15,700 and introduced capital of $2,750. Ronnie made a profit for the year of $13,800.

What was Ronnie's capital account balance at the start of the accounting year?

$

276 Andi works as a joiner. At 1 July 20X5 Andi had a capital account balance of $12,735. During the year, Andi made withdrawals from the business for own use of $2,345, and had a capital account balance of $2,690 at 30 June 20X6.

What was Andi's loss for the year ended 30 June 20X6?

$

277 On 1 July 20X5 Luca introduced capital of $7,500 into the business and also raised a loan from the bank for the same amount at an interest rate of 8% per annum, payable annually in arrears.

How should this information be classified in the statement of financial position at 31 December 20X5?

A Business liabilities of $15,300

B Proprietor's capital of $7,500 and business liabilities of $7,500

C Proprietor's capital of $7,500 and business liabilities of $7,800

D Proprietor's capital of $15,000

278 Nayan, a sole trader, had an opening capital balance of $28,350 and a closing capital balance of $25,685. In addition, Nayan made a profit for the year of $9,335 and introduced capital of $3,000.

What were Nayan's drawings from the business for the year?

$

279 Lochan had opening capital of $18,500 and closing capital of $16,750. During the year, Lochan made a loss of $8,000 withdrew $8,500 for own use.

How much capital did Lochan introduce during the year?

$

280 **What is the correct accounting treatment of finance costs accrued on a loan taken out by Mitch during the year?**

A	Debit: Drawings, and	Credit: Capital
B	Debit: Capital, and	Credit: Profit or loss
C	Debit: Profit or loss, and	Credit: Liabilities
D	Debit: Profit or loss, and	Credit: Bank

RECONCILIATIONS

281 Nibaal is preparing the bank reconciliation and noted the following:

(i) the bank levied charges on the account

(ii) a cheque payable to S. Wright (a supplier) has not been presented at the bank.

Which of the above errors require an entry in Nibaal's bank general ledger account?

A both (i) and (ii)

B (i) only

C neither (i) nor (ii)

D (ii) only

282 When Nimat checked the entries in the bank general ledger account with the bank statement seven cheques with a total value of $3,259 had not been presented at the bank. Nimat had instructed the bank to cancel two of these cheques, but did not make any entries in the general ledger. The value of the cancelled cheques is $642.

What entry should Nimat make in the bank general ledger account to correct the balance?

A Debit $642

B Debit $2,617

C Credit $642

D Credit $2,617

283 The following attempt at a bank reconciliation statement has been prepared by a member of the accounts staff at T Co:

	$
Overdraft per bank statement	38,600
Add: deposits not credited	41,200
	79,800
Less: outstanding cheques	3,300
Overdraft per bank ledger account	$76,500

Assuming that the bank statement balance of $38,600 was correct, what was the correct credit balance per the bank ledger account?

$

284 **After checking the bank ledger account against the bank statement, which TWO of the following four items could require an entry in the bank general ledger account?**

	Selected answer
Bank charges	
Cheque not presented	
A dishonoured cheque from a customer	
Deposits not credited	

285 Lin found the following when carrying out the bank reconciliation:

(i) a cheque for $7,523 has not been presented at the bank

(ii) a cheque for $560 has been incorrectly recorded as $650 in Lin's bank general ledger.

Which of these items will require an entry in Lin's bank general ledger account?

A (i) only

B (ii) only

C Both (i) and (ii)

D Neither (i) nor (ii)

286 Jodie is carrying out a reconciliation of the bank account in the general ledger with the balance per the bank statement.

Jodie found the following reasons for the difference between the two balances:

(i) Several cheques paid to suppliers have not been presented at the bank.

(ii) The bank levied charges on Jodie's account.

(iii) A customer paid $980 directly into Jodie's bank account.

Which of the above items will require an entry in the general ledger?

A (i) and (ii) only

B (ii) and (iii) only

C (i) and (iii) only

D (i), (ii) and (iii)

287 You are preparing a client's final accounts. You know that the client's bookkeeper has correctly completed a reconciliation of the bank balance in the general ledger to the balance on the bank statement. The balances from the general ledger and the bank statement were:

General ledger balance $2,358 (credit) Bank statement balance $1,053 (debit)

The difference between the two account balances is explained by unpresented cheques and outstanding lodgements.

How should the bank balance be reported in the final accounts?

A As a current asset of $1,053

B As a current liability of $1,053

C As a current asset of $2,358

D As a current liability of $2,358

288 Jeb prepared the bank reconciliation, using the balance in the general ledger of $422 credit. The only items which needed to be considered were:

(i) a cheque for $822 issued to a supplier which has not yet appeared on the bank statement

(ii) interest received of $153 which was credited by the bank, but not recorded by Jeb.

What was the closing balance on Jeb's bank statement?

A $269 overdrawn

B $1,091 overdrawn

C $553 cash at bank

D $1,197 cash at bank

289 At 30 April 20X8 the bank account balance in Jital's general ledger showed that there was $685 cash at the bank. When Jital prepared the bank reconciliation, it was discovered that bank charges of $722 for the year to 30 April 20X8 had been omitted.

What cash at bank balance should be included on Jital's opening trial balance at 1 May 20X8?

A $685 debit

B $685 credit

C $37 debit

D $37 credit

290 Phip's bank reconciliation statement shows outstanding lodgements paid in of $3,800 and outstanding cheques to suppliers of $3,500. Phip's bank account in the general ledger shows a debit balance of $25,000.

What balance does Phip's bank statement show?

A $25,000

B $24,700

C $25,300

D $32,300

291 The following attempt at a bank reconciliation statement was prepared by Shi:

	$
Overdraft per bank statement	38,600
Add: deposits not credited	41,200
	79,800
Less: outstanding cheques	3,300
Overdraft per bank ledger account	$76,500

Assuming the bank statement balance of $38,600 is correct, what should the bank ledger account balance be?

A $76,500 overdrawn

B $5,900 overdrawn

C $700 overdrawn

D $5,900 cash at bank

292 The balance on the bank ledger account of a business at 30 June was an overdraft of $89.93. At that date there were also unpresented cheques totalling $154.38 and an outstanding deposit of $60.00. It was also discovered that during the month of June the bank had charged the business interest on its overdraft for the previous quarter of $16.45.

What is the correct balance on the bank ledger account at the end of June?

A $73.48 overdrawn

B $106.38 overdrawn

C $167.86 overdrawn

D $200.76 overdrawn

293 A business has a debit balance in its bank general ledger account of $148.00 but the bank statement shows a different balance. The following items have also been discovered:

(i) the bank statement shows that there were bank charges for the period of $10 which have not been recorded in the bank ledger account

(ii) a standing order payment for $25 has also been mistakenly omitted from the bank ledger account

(iii) cheques totalling $125 had been written and sent to suppliers but had not yet been presented

(iv) a cheque for $85 had been paid into the bank but was still outstanding

What is the balance on the bank statement?

A $73

B $113

C $153

D $223

294 The bank statement shows an overdraft of $210. Uncredited lodgements are $30 and unpresented cheques are $83. A dishonoured cheque for $28 was included in the bank statement but has not yet been recorded in the bank ledger account.

What is the correct bank ledger account balance?

A $263 overdrawn

B $235 overdrawn

C $157 overdrawn

D $129 overdrawn

295 The bank statement shows a balance at the bank of $1,360, whilst the bank general ledger account balance on the same date is $1,250.

How could this discrepancy be explained?

A Uncredited lodgement of $110

B Bank charges of $110 not yet recorded in the general ledger account

C Bank interest received of $55 credited in the general ledger account

D A dishonoured cheque for $55 which the business did not know about until it was returned, after the date of the bank statement

296 What is the purpose of performing a bank reconciliation?

A The reconciliation confirms that the bank statement balance is correct

B The reconciliation confirms that all transactions in the bank general ledger account have been processed through the bank account, with any reconciling items properly accounted for

C The reconciliation confirms that there are no errors in the bank general ledger account

D The reconciliation confirms that there are no errors within the bank statement

297 Consider the following statements relating to bank reconciliations:

Is each statement true or false?

	True	**False**
If the bank statement balance and bank general ledger account balance is not identical as at a specific date, it means that there must be one or more errors in the general ledger account.		
If the bank statement balance and bank general ledger account balance is not identical as at a specific date, it means that there must be one or more errors in the bank statement.		

298 A supplier issues a statement to Pen Co showing a balance outstanding of $14,350. Pen Co's own records show a balance outstanding of $14,500.

What could be a possible reason for this situation?

A The supplier sent an invoice for $150 which Pen Co has not yet received

B The supplier has allowed Pen Co $150 cash discount which is not yet recorded in the general ledger

C Pen Co has paid the supplier $150 who has not yet accounted for the cash receipt

D Pen Co has returned goods worth $150 which the supplier has not yet accounted for

299 ANO Co issued a supplier statement to BNO Co showing a balance outstanding of $14,350. BNO Co's records show a balance outstanding of $14,500.

From BNO Co's perspective, which of the following statements could be a reason that explains this difference?

A The supplier issued an invoice for $150 which BNO Co has not yet received

B The supplier has allowed BNO Co $150 cash discount which has not yet been recorded in the general ledger accounts

C BNO Co has paid the supplier $150 who has not yet accounted for the cash receipt

D BNO Co has returned goods worth $150 which the supplier has not yet accounted for

300 **Which of the following would be identified by matching a supplier statement against the transactions within the month?**

A Incorrect calculations on invoices

B Non-delivery of goods charged

C Incorrect trade discounts

D Duplication of invoices

301 A supplier issued a statement of account to Spark Co showing a balance outstanding of $2,850 at 28 February 20X3. Spark Co's payables ledger account for that supplier had a balance of $2,925.

Which of the following reasons could account for this difference?

A Spark Co has paid the supplier $75 which has not yet been received and accounted for by the supplier

B Spark Co has returned goods of $75 which the supplier has not yet accounted for

C The supplier has allowed Spark Co settlement discount of $75 which Spark Co has not yet accounted for in its accounting records

D The supplier issued an invoice for $75 that Spark Co has not yet received

302 Ordan received a statement from one of its suppliers, Alta, showing a balance due of $3,980. The amount due according to the payables' ledger account of Ordan was only $230.

Comparison of the statement and the ledger account revealed the following differences:

1. A cheque sent by Ordan for $270 has not been recorded in Alta's statement.
2. Alta has not recorded goods returned by Ordan $180.
3. Ordan made a contra entry, reducing the amount due to Alta by $3,200, for a balance due from Alta in Ordan's receivables ledger. No such entry has been made in Alta's records.

What difference remains between the two entities' accounting records after adjusting for these items?

A $460

B $640

C $6,500

D $100

303 A supplier sent Lee Co a statement showing a balance outstanding of $14,350. Lee Co's records show a balance outstanding of $14,500.

Which of the following reasons could account for this difference?

A The supplier sent an invoice for $150 which Lee Co has not yet received

B The supplier has allowed Lee Co $150 settlement discount which Lee Co has not yet accounted for in its accounting records

C Lee Co has paid the supplier $150 which has not yet been accounted for by the supplier

D Lee Co has returned goods of $150 which the supplier has not yet accounted for

304 Tarbuck Co received a statement of account from one of its suppliers, showing an outstanding balance due to it of $1,350. On comparison with the payable ledger account, the following was identified:

1. The ledger account shows a credit balance of $260.
2. The supplier has disallowed a cash discount of $80 due to late payment of an invoice.
3. The supplier has not yet allowed for goods returned at the end of the period of $270.
4. Cash in transit of $830 has not been received by the supplier.

Following consideration of these items, what was the unreconciled difference between the statement of account from the supplier and Tarbuck Co's payable ledger account?

A $70

B $90

C $430

D $590

305 Who issues a statement of account and why is it issued?

A A business issues a statement of account to those suppliers it still owes money to, advising them of the amount outstanding

B A business issues a statement of account to cash customers to advise them how much they have purchased in the previous month

C A business issues a statement of account to credit customers to advise them how much the customer owes the business

D A business issues a statement of account to all credit customers and suppliers to advise them of the amount outstanding or due

306 Which of the following statements relating to a statement of account issued by a supplier to a customer is true?

A The balance on a statement of account will always agree with the payable ledger account balance of the customer

B The balance on a statement of account will never agree with the payable ledger account balance of the customer

C The balance on a statement of account will always be higher than the payable ledger account balance of the customer

D The balance on a statement of account can be agreed or reconciled with the payable ledger account balance of the customer subject to identification of goods in transit, cash in transit, early settlement discount or goods returned

307 Rome Co received a statement from one of its suppliers, Alpha, showing a balance due of \$3,465 at 30 April 20X4.

Upon reviewing the payables ledger account and the supplier statement the following differences were identified:

1 An automated payment for \$690 was not recorded on the statement from Alpha.

2 Rome Co had not recorded an invoice issued by Alpha on 29 April 20X4 for \$280.

What was the payable ledger account balance at 30 April 20X4 for Alpha maintained by Rome Co?

A \$4,435

B \$3,875

C \$2,495

D \$3,055

308 Milan Co received a statement dated 30 November 20X7 from one of its suppliers, Beta, showing a balance due of $4,278.

Upon reviewing the payables ledger account and the supplier statement the following differences were identified:

1 A contra of $784 recently agreed with Beta was not recorded on the statement from Beta.

2 Milan Co had not recorded an invoice issued on 29 November by Beta for $543.

When all transactions have been recorded, what will be the updated balance on the payable ledger account for Beta maintained by Milan Co?

A $5,342

B $4,782

C $3,214

D $3,494

309 Delta issued a statement to one of its customers, Verona Co for the month ended 31 January 20X2. At that date, the payable ledger account for Delta maintained by Verona Co had a balance of $6,045.

A review of Verona Co's payable ledger account for Delta and the supplier statement revealed the following differences:

1 Verona Co had recorded discount received of $25 along with a payment made of $389 which was not recorded on the statement.

2 Verona Co had returned goods which cost $105 which was not yet recorded on the statement.

What was the balance on the statement at 31 January 20X2 issued by Delta?

A $6,564

B $6,539

C $6,434

D $5,526

310 Zeta issued a statement to one of its customers, Portofino Co for the month of July 20X4. At 31 July 20X4, the payable ledger account for Zeta maintained by Portofino Co had a balance of $7,672.

A review of Portofino Co's payable ledger account for Zeta and the supplier statement revealed the following differences:

1 Portofino Co had not yet recorded a purchase invoice from Zeta for goods which cost $435.

2 Portofino Co made an automated payment of $1,506 on 30 July 20X4 which was not recorded on the statement.

What was the closing balance on the statement issued by Zeta?

A $9,178

B $5,731

C $9,613

D $6,601

311 Genoa Co received a statement for the month ended 30 April 20X3 from one of its suppliers, Theta, showing a balance due of $4,278.

Upon reviewing the payables ledger account and the supplier statement the following differences were identified:

1 A contra of $784 recently agreed with Theta was not recorded on the statement from Beta.

2 Genoa Co had not recorded an invoice issued by Theta for $543.

What was the balance on the payable ledger account for Theta maintained by Genoa Co at 30 April 20X3?

A $4,519

B $5,605

C $3,494

D $2,951

312 Kappa issued a statement to one of its customers, Venice Co for the month ended 31 May 20X8. The payable ledger account for Kappa maintained by Venice Co had a balance of $4,368.

A review of Venice Co's payable ledger account for Kappa and the supplier statement revealed the following differences:

1 Venice Co had recorded discount received of $22 along with an automated bank payment made of $389. Only the bank payment was recorded on the statement. Discussion with Kappa identified that the payment was received late and that the discount would not be granted.

2 Venice Co had returned goods which cost $532 which was not yet recorded on the statement.

What was the closing balance at 31 May 20X8 on the statement issued by Kappa?

A $4,922

B $4,408

C $3,858

D $3,814

313 Lecce Co received a statement dated 30 September 20X5 from one of its suppliers, Rho, showing a balance due of $7,278.

Upon reviewing the payables ledger account and the supplier statement the following differences were identified:

1 A contra of $2,471 recently agreed with Rho was not recorded on the statement from Rho.

2 Lecce Co had not recorded a credit note issued by Rho on 29 September for $832.

What is the payable ledger account balance at 30 September 20X5 for Rho as maintained by Lecce Co?

A $3,168

B $6,446

C $4,807

D $5,639

314 Parma Co received a statement for the month ended 31 March 20X3 from one of its suppliers, Sigma, showing a balance due of $4,684.

Upon reviewing the payables ledger account and the supplier statement the following differences were identified:

1. Parma Co had not recorded an invoice issued by Sigma for $584, and nor had it recorded a credit note issued by Sigma for $276.
2. An automated bank payment of $1,342 made recently was not recorded on the statement from Sigma.

When all transactions have been recorded, what will be the updated payable ledger account balance for Sigma maintained by Parma Co at 31 March 20X3?

A $3,034

B $3,342

C $3,650

D $2,482

315 Omega issued a statement to one of its customers, Turin Co for the month ended 31 October 20X9. At that date, the payable ledger account for Omega maintained by Turin Co had a balance of $1,213.

A review of Turin Co's payable ledger account for Omega and the supplier statement revealed the following differences:

1. Turin Co had not recorded an invoice for $241 or a credit note for $92 recently issued by Omega.
2. Turin Co agreed a contra with Omega of $421 which was not yet recorded on the statement.

What was the balance on the statement issued by Omega for the month ended 31 October 20X9?

A $792

B $1,362

C $1,783

D $941

316 Tau issued a statement to one of its customers, Ancona Co for the month ended 28 February 20X5. At that date, the payable ledger account for Tau maintained by Ancona Co had a balance of $4,575.

A review of Ancona Co's payable ledger account for Tau and the supplier statement revealed the following differences:

1 Ancona Co had not recorded a credit note for $18 recently issued by Tau.

2 An invoice on the statement from Tau for $875 related to another customer and had been included in in error.

What was the balance on the statement issued by Tau for the month ended 31 October 20X9?

A $4,557

B $5,432

C $4,593

D $3,682

317 Omicron issued a statement to one of its customers, Bologna Co for the month ended 28 February 20X5 with a closing balance of $8,314.

A review of Bologna Co's payable ledger account for Omicron and the supplier statement revealed the following differences:

1 Bologna Co made an automated payment of $2,546 on 27 February 20X5 which was not recorded on the statement issued by Omicron.

2 An invoice on the payable ledger account for Omicron for $1,456 related to another supplier and had been recorded in Omicron's payable ledger account in error.

What was the initial payable ledger account balance for Omicron as maintained by Bologna Co for the month ended 28 February 20X9?

A $7,224

B $5,768

C $4,678

D $6,134

318 Following a reconciliation of the most recent statement received from a supplier, Omicron, Bologna Co discovered that a purchase invoice from Omega had been allocated to the payable ledger account of Omicron.

What accounting entries should Bologna Co record to rectify this error?

A	Debit: Payables, and	Credit: Purchases
B	Debit: Purchases, and	Credit: Payables
C	Debit: Payable ledger Omicron, and	Credit: Payable ledger Omega
D	Debit: Payable ledger Omega, and	Credit: Payable ledger Omicron

319 Following a reconciliation of the most recent statement received from a supplier, Kappa, Venice Co discovered that discount received of $22 it had recorded had not been allowed by Kappa.

What accounting entries in the general ledger should Venice Co record to rectify this error?

A	Debit: Payable ledger – Kappa $22, and	Credit: Payables $22
B	Debit: Discount received $22, and	Credit: Payable ledger – Kappa 22
C	Debit: Payables $22, and	Credit: Discount received $22
D	Debit: Discount received $22, and	Credit: Payables $22

320 The payables account for the year ended 31 May 20X7 in Lisbon Co's general ledger is presented below.

Payables

	$		$
Contra with receivables	3,925	Balance	37,500
Bank	340,750	Purchases	357,500
Discount received	1,325		
Returns outwards	11,235		
Balance	37,765		
	395,000		395,000

What numerical value should be included in the statement of financial position as at 31 May 20X7 within liabilities?

A $37,500

B $37,765

C $395,000

D $357,500

321 Phi issued a statement to one of its customers, Trento Co for the month of August 20X4. At 31 August 20X4, the payable ledger account for Phi maintained by Trento Co had a balance of $6,727.

A review of Trento Co's payable ledger account for Phi and the supplier statement revealed the following differences:

1 Trento Co had not yet recorded a purchase invoice of $534 from Phi.

2 Trento Co made an automated payment of $1,605 on 30 August 20X4 which was not recorded on the statement.

What was the closing balance on the statement issued by Phi?

A $7,798

B $8,332

C $8,866

D $5,122

THE TRIAL BALANCE AND CORRECTION OF ERRORS

322 Which of the following statements regarding the trial balance is/are correct?

(i) If the total of the debit balances equals the total of the credit balances, no errors have been made in posting to the general ledger.

(ii) The trial balance always records non-current assets at market value.

A (i) only

B (ii) only

C Both (i) and (ii)

D Neither (i) nor (ii)

323 Which of the following are limitations of the trial balance?

1 It does not include all final figures to be included in the financial statements.

2 It does not identify all errors of commission.

3 It does not identify in which accounts errors have been made.

A 1 and 2 only

B 2 and 3 only

C 1, 2 and 3

D 1 and 3 only

324 Identify whether each of the following statements is true or false.

	True	**False**
The trial balance provides a check that no errors exist in the accounting records of a business.		
The trial balance is one of the financial statements prepared annually by an entity for its shareholders.		

325 Which one of the following errors could not occur in a computerised accounting system?

A Reversal of accounting entries

B Error of omission

C Error of principle

D An arithmetic error on a general ledger account in arriving at the account balance

326 What is the purpose of producing a trial balance?

A It confirms the profit made for the year

B It confirms that an equal value of debits and credits have been posted in the general ledger during the accounting period

C It confirms that there are no duplicated transactions in the general ledger

D It confirms that there are no transactions have been omitted from the general ledger

327 When processing an expense invoice in the accounting system, Maxi correctly recorded the payable liability but debited the motor expenses account, rather than the insurance account.

What type of error is this?

A Error of commission

B Error of principle

C Reversal of entries

D Compensating error

328 When processing an invoice for the purchase of a new motor, Maxi correctly recorded the payable liability but debited the motor expenses account, rather than the motors non-current asset account.

What type of error is this?

A Reversal of entries

B Compensating error

C Error of principle

D Error of commission

329 In which columns in the trial balance should the following general ledger accounts be included?

	Sales returns	**Purchases returns**
A	Debit	Debit
B	Debit	Credit
C	Credit	Debit
D	Credit	Credit

330 In which columns in the trial balance should the following general ledger accounts be included?

	Irrecoverable debts	**Discount received**
A	Debit	Debit
B	Debit	Credit
C	Credit	Debit
D	Credit	Credit

331 In which columns in the trial balance should the following general ledger accounts be included?

	Allowance for receivables	Bank overdraft
A	Debit	Debit
B	Debit	Credit
C	Credit	Debit
D	Credit	Credit

332 Which group of general ledger accounts includes an account which is a debit balance?

A Bank overdraft, sales tax receivable, accruals

B Returns outwards, buildings at cost, discount received

C Sales, allowance for receivables, sales tax payable

D Bank overdraft, accumulated depreciation, payables

333 Which group of general ledger accounts includes an account which is a credit balance?

A Insurance, machinery at cost, sales tax recoverable

B Wages, Carriage outwards, carriage inwards

C Prepayments, capital account, purchases

D Opening inventory, irrecoverable debts, rent

334 After completing the final accounts, Kai found that a prepayment was understated.

How are Kai's net profit and capital affected by correction of this error?

	Net profit	Capital
A	Increased	Increased
B	Increased	Decreased
C	Decreased	Increased
D	Decreased	Decreased

335 When recording purchase invoices in the accounting system, Murali recorded an invoice for \$126 for motor repairs as \$162.

What accounting entries are required to correct this error?

	Debit	Credit
A	Motor expenses \$36	Payables \$36
B	Payables \$36	Motor expenses \$36
C	Motor expenses \$288	Payables \$288
D	Payables \$288	Motor expenses \$288

336 Consider the following statements relating to suspense accounts:

Is each statement true or false?

	True	**False**
A separate suspense account should be opened for each error in the general ledger		
A suspense account is sometimes opened to complete postings whilst more information is sought on a transaction		

337 Pahal's trial balance includes a temporary suspense account with a balance of $280 relating to settlement discount on early payment of an amount due to a credit supplier. The accounting entry in the payables' account had been correctly recorded in the general ledger but the junior accountant was unsure where to record the other half of the transaction and posted it to suspense account pending further guidance.

What are the accounting entries required to clear the suspense account?

A Debit: Suspense, and Credit: Sales

B Debit: Discount received, and Credit: Suspense

C Debit: Suspense, and Credit: Discount received

D Debit: Sales, and Credit: Suspense

338 Georgie is preparing the general ledger journal entry to write off an irrecoverable debt. Georgie knows that the debit entry should be made in the receivables expense account and posted the other part of the transaction to a temporary suspense account pending further enquiries.

Into which general ledger account should Georgie have posted the credit entry?

A Sales account

B Bank account

C Receivables account

D Receivables allowance account

339 Daz is preparing the general ledger journal entry to record discount received. The transaction was properly recorded in the payables account, with the other entry recorded in\temporary suspense account to clarify how it should be recorded in the general ledger.

What accounting entries should be made to clear the suspense account and record the transaction correctly?

A Debit Receivables, and Credit Suspense

B Debit Discount received, and Credit Suspense

C Debit Suspense, and Credit Purchases

D Debit Suspense, and Credit Discount received

340 Smart Co had a temporary suspense account balance of $9,000 in its general ledger. This balance related to the proceeds of disposal of a non-current asset. The proceeds had been correctly recorded in the cash at bank account but the accounts clerk was unsure of the other accounting entry required and posted it to the suspense account pending further enquiries.

What accounting entries are required to clear the suspense account?

A	Dr Non-current assets – cost $9,000	Cr Suspense $9,000
B	Dr Disposal of non-current asset $9,000	Cr Suspense $9,000
C	Dr Suspense $9,000	Cr Disposal of non-current asset $9,000
D	Dr Suspense $9,000	Cr Non-current assets – cost $9,000

341 Savvy Co had a temporary suspense account balance of $1,300 in its general ledger. This balance related to the accounting for an increase in the allowance for receivables. The increase in the allowance had been correctly recorded in the allowance for receivables account but the other accounting entry was posted to the suspense account pending the junior accountant making further enquiries.

What accounting entries are required to clear the suspense account?

A	Dr Irrecoverable debts expense $1,300	Cr Suspense $1,300
B	Dr Receivables $1,300	Cr Suspense $9,000
C	Dr Suspense $1,300	Cr Receivables $1,300
D	Dr Suspense $1,300	Cr Irrecoverable debts expense $1,300

342 A trial balance for Walker Co was extracted as at 31 December 20X3, and the account balances have been grouped into those relating to the statement of profit or loss or the statement of financial position as follows:

	Debit balances	**Credit balances**
Statement of financial position	$136,778	$86,677
Statement of profit or loss	$231,816	$281,917

What is Walker Co's profit for the year ended 31 December 20X3?

$

343 Runner Co's general ledger account balances in the trial balance have been separated into those relating to the statement of profit or loss or the statement of financial position as follows:

	Debit balances	**Credit balances**
Statement of profit or loss	148,990	136,909
Statement of financial position	149.608	161,689

What is Runner Co's loss for the year?

$

344 Jose identified two issues when reviewing the computerised general ledger accounts and other financial information of the business as follows:

Error

1 $360 received from Brown, a credit customer, was credited in error to the account of Green, another credit customer.

2 No entries had been made to record a cash sale of $100.

Which of the errors above would require an entry to the suspense account as part of the process of correcting them?

A Neither error 1, nor error 2

B Error 1 only

C Both Error 1 and error 2

D Error 2 only

345 Delta identified two issues when reviewing the computerised general ledger accounts and other financial information of the business as follows:

Error

1 The depreciation charge for the year had been debited to the irrecoverable debts account. The other part of the accounting entry had been made correctly.

2 Some of the cash receipts from customers had been used to pay sundry expenses before banking the money and had not been recorded.

Which of the above errors would require an entry to the suspense account as part of the process of correcting them?

A Error 1 only

B Neither error 1, nor error 2

C Both Error 1 and error 2

D Error 2 only

346 Two common types of error in bookkeeping are:

- an error of principle
- an error of transposition.

Which of the following correctly states whether or not these errors will be revealed by extracting a trial balance?

	Errors of principle	**Errors of transposition**
A	Will be revealed	Will **not** be revealed
B	Will be revealed	Will be revealed
C	Will **not** be revealed	Will **not** be revealed
D	Will **not** be revealed	Will be revealed

347 Dalbir extracted the following list of balances from the general ledger at 31 October 20X5:

	$
Sales	258,542
Opening inventory	9,649
Purchases	142,958
Expenses	34,835
Non-current assets at carrying amount	63,960
Receivables	31,746
Payables	13,864
Cash at bank	1,783
Capital	12,525

What is the total of the debit balances in Dalbir's trial balance at 31 October 20X5?

A $267,049

B $275,282

C $283,148

D $284,931

348 When Sprout Co's trial balance was extended and totalled, the totals were:

	Debit balances	**Credit balances**
Statement of profit or loss	$97,945	$120,634
Statement of financial position	$84,752	$62,063

What is Sprout Co's profit or loss for the year?

A $22,689 loss

B $22,689 profit

C $35,882 loss

D $35,882 profit

349 When recording the purchase of goods from a credit supplier, Lime Co posted the gross cost of $1,500 to the purchases and payables general ledger accounts. Both the supplier and Lime Co are registered to account for sales tax at the rate of 20%.

What journal adjustment should Lime Co make to correct this error?

A	Dr	Purchases	$300, and	Cr	Sales tax	$300
B	Dr	Sales tax	$250, and	Cr	Purchases	$250
C	Dr	Sales tax	$300, and	Cr	Purchases	$300
D	Dr	Purchases	$250, and	Cr	Sales tax	$250

350 Peach Co returned faulty goods to a supplier and received a credit note from the supplier. When recording the credit note in the accounting system, Lime Co omitted to account for sales tax and, instead posted the gross amount of $1,296 to the returns outwards account. Both Peach Co and the supplier are registered to account for sales tax at the rate of 8%.

What journal adjustment should Peach Co make to correct this error?

A	Dr	Sales tax	$96, and	Cr	Cash at bank	$300
B	Dr	Sales tax	$96, and	Cr	Payables	$250
C	Dr	Sales tax	$96, and	Cr	Returns outwards	$96
D	Dr	Sales tax	$96, and	Cr	Purchases	$250

351 When recording a contra entry for $2,000 in the general ledger, Lemon Co correctly recorded the entry in the payables account, and recorded the other entry in the allowance for receivables account. Both Lemon and Co and the other party are registered to account for sales tax at the rate of 20%.

What journal adjustment should Lemon Co make to correct this error?

A Dr Receivables $2,000, and Cr Allowance for receivables $2,000

B Dr Receivables $2,400, and Cr Receivables $2,400

C Dr Allowance for receivables $2,400, and Cr Receivables $2,400

D Dr Allowance for receivables $2,000, and Cr Receivables $2,000

352 When recording a purchase invoice for the repair of a laptop from a credit supplier, Orange Co recorded it as an addition to non-current assets. The cost of the repair was $500, on which sales tax was charged at 15%. Orange Co is registered to account for sales tax.

What journal adjustment should Orange Co make to correct this error?

A Dr Repairs $500, and Cr Non-current assets $500

B Dr Repairs $575, and Cr Non-current assets $575

C Dr Non-current assets $500, and Cr Repairs $500

D Dr Non-current assets $575, and Cr Repairs $575

353 When recording a sales invoice for a credit customer, Date Co recorded the net amount as $1,000 instead of $100. Date Co is registered to account for sales tax at 10%.

What journal adjustment should Date Co make to correct this error?

A	Dr	Repairs	$500, and	Cr	Non-current assets	$500
B	Dr	Repairs	$575, and	Cr	Non-current assets	$575
C	Dr	Non-current assets $500, and		Cr	Repairs	$500
D	Dr	Sales	$900, and	Cr	Receivables	$990
	Dr	Sales tax	$90			

354 Tangerine Co made a sale to a credit customer for $500 plus sales tax at 40% which was recorded correctly in the general ledger. The customer subsequently returned half of the goods as they were damaged upon receipt and a credit note was issued for that amount. The entry for the credit note in the receivables account was made correctly and the other entry was made for the same amount in the returns inwards account.

What journal adjustment should Tangerine Co make to correct this error?

A	Dr	Returns inwards $50, and	Cr	Sales tax	$50
B	Dr	Sales tax $50, and	Cr	Returns inwards	$50
C	Dr	Sales tax $100, and	Cr	Returns inwards	$100
D	Dr	Returns inwards $100, and	Cr	Sales tax	$100

355 When recording a purchase invoice for the purchase of a grating machine, Satsuma Co recorded it as a machine repair. The cost of the machine was $5,000, on which sales tax was charged at 15%. Satsuma Co is registered to account for sales tax.

What journal adjustment should Satsuma make to correct this error?

A	Dr	Repairs $5,000, and Sales tax $750	Cr	Non-current assets	$5,750
B	Dr	Repairs $5,750 and	Cr	Non-current assets	$5,750
C	Dr	Non-current assets $5,000, and	Cr	Repairs	$5,000
D	Dr	Non-current assets $5,750, and	Cr	Repairs	$5,750

PREPARING FINANCIAL STATEMENTS

356 Punit extracted a trial balance which included ledger account balances for depreciation expense and accumulated depreciation.

How should these ledger account balances be included in the financial statements?

	Depreciation expense	**Accumulated depreciation**
A	Profit or loss statement debit	Profit or loss statement credit
B	Statement of financial position credit	Statement of financial position debit
C	Profit or loss statement debit	Statement of financial position credit
D	Statement of financial position debit	Profit or loss statement credit

357 The trial balance of Crew Co included ledger account balances for irrecoverable debts and the allowance for receivables.

How should these ledger account balances be included in the financial statements?

	Allowance for receivables	**Irrecoverable debts**
A	Profit or loss statement debit	Profit or loss statement credit
B	Statement of financial position credit	Statement of financial position debit
C	Profit or loss statement debit	Statement of financial position credit
D	Statement of financial position debit	Profit or loss statement credit

358 Jiva has been advised that a customer has ceased trading and that it is almost certain that the balance due of $720 will not be recovered.

What adjustment is required to write off this amount in the financial statements?

	Debit	**Credit**
A	Receivables	Irrecoverable debts
B	Irrecoverable debts	Receivables
C	Receivables	Bank
D	Bank	Receivables

359 At 30 April 20X7 the total amount owed to Joginder by customers was $54,864. At the same date, Joginder calculated that the receivables allowance was $3,775.

How should these balances be reported in Joginder's statement of financial position?

A $51,089 as a current asset

B $51,089 as a current liability

C $54,864 as a current asset, and $3,775 as a current liability

D $54,864 as a current liability, and $3,775 as a current asset

360 Kahali calculated that the receivables allowance at 30 April 20X7 should be $890. At 1 May 20X6, Kahali's receivables allowance was $770.

How should the movement in the receivables allowance be recorded in Kahali's statement of profit or loss?

A A charge of $890

B A credit of $890

C A charge of $120

D A credit of $120

361 An irrecoverable debt of $1,500 that was written off two years ago was unexpectedly recovered and entered in the receivables in the general ledger.

What accounting entries are required, assuming that the receipt was treated as a receipt from a current receivable, to correctly account for this receipt?

	Debit	**Credit**
A	Irrecoverable debts	Trade receivables
B	Receivables	Irrecoverable debts
C	Suspense account	Irrecoverable debts account
D	No adjustment will be necessary	

362 Syl's financial year ended on 30 November 20X2. The last invoice paid for telephone calls was for $1,800. This invoice covered the three months to 31 October 20X2.

What adjustment is required when preparing the accounts for the year to 30 November 20X2?

A A prepayment of $600

B A prepayment of $1,200

C An accrual of $600

D An accrual of $1,200

363 Raman prepared draft final accounts, which show a net profit of $24,952 and closing capital of $75,841. Raman has now found that a supplier's invoice for $250 for advertising expenses was not recorded in the general ledger.

When the error is corrected, what are the revised balances for net profit and capital?

	Net profit	**Capital**
A	$24,702	$75,591
B	$24,702	$76,091
C	$25,202	$75,591
D	$25,202	$76,091

364 The accountant at Carter Co has obtained the trial balance and is now preparing the financial statements for the year ended 30 November 20X6.

How should the inventory valuation at 30 November 20X6 be included in the financial statements?

A Profit or loss statement debit and profit or loss statement credit

B Statement of financial position debit and statement of financial position credit

C Profit or loss statement debit and statement of financial position credit

D Profit or loss statement credit and statement of financial position debit

365 Satya is preparing the financial statements for the year ended 30 June 20X3.

How should the annual depreciation charge and the accumulated depreciation be included in the financial statements?

	Depreciation charge	**Accumulated depreciation**
A	Profit or loss statement debit	Statement of financial position debit
B	Profit or loss statement debit	Statement of financial position credit
C	profit or loss statement credit	Statement of financial position credit
D	Profit or loss statement credit	Statement of financial position debit

366 Jed's electricity expense account has a debit balance of $1,540. Jed had no opening accrual or prepayment for electricity. The last electricity invoice was for $462 for the three months to 30 September 20X7.

What are the correct amounts to be charged to Jed's statement of profit or loss for the year to 30 November 20X7 and reported as an accrual in the statement of financial position at 30 November 20X7 for electricity?

	Profit or loss charge	Accrual
A	$1,694	$154
B	$1,694	$308
C	$1,848	$154
D	$1,848	$308

367 On 1 December 20X6 Pat borrowed $40,000 at a fixed rate of interest. A single capital repayment is due on 1 December 20X9. During the year to 30 November 20X7, the interest of $300 per month was paid on the last day of each month.

How should the loan liability be reported on Pat's statement of financial position at 30 November 20X7?

	Current liability	Non-current liability
A	$3,600	$40,000
B	$40,000	$3,600
C	Nil	$40,000
D	$40,000	Nil

The following information relates to questions 368 and 369.

At 31 May 20X8, Sonu's general ledger included the following balances:

Trade receivables	$137,850
Receivables allowance at 1 June 20X7	$2,492

Sonu calculated that the receivables' allowance should be revised to $2,757.

Note: in the exam, all questions will be independent, and not based on a common scenario.

368 **What amount should be reported in Sonu's profit or loss for the change to the allowance for receivables?**

A a charge of $265

B a credit of $265

C a charge of $2,757

D a credit of $2,757

369 How should receivables be reported in Sonu's statement of financial position at 31 May 20X8?

A Current asset of $137,850 and current liability of $2,757

B Current asset of $135,093

C Current asset of $137,850 and current liability of $2,492

D Current asset of $135,358

370 Which one of the following items should be included in the calculation of gross profit?

A Carriage inwards

B Carriage outwards

C Irrecoverable debts written off

D An increase in the allowance for receivables

371 After Toni prepared the draft accounts it was discovered that an item of expense had been incorrectly classified an item of asset expenditure.

When the error is corrected, how will Toni's net profit and capital be affected?

	Net profit	**Capital**
A	Increased	Reduced
B	Reduced	Increased
C	Increased	Increased
D	Reduced	Reduced

372 How should each of the following items be classified in the financial statements?

	Current asset	**Non-current asset**
Assets which will be converted into cash as part of normal business activity		
Assets which are used to increase productive capacity of the business		

373 On 1 November 20X4 Lex took out a business development loan of $30,000. The loan is to be repaid in ten equal six-monthly instalments. Lex made the first repayment of $3,000 on 1 May 20X5.

How should the outstanding balance of $27,000 be reported on Lex's statement of financial position at 31 May 20X5?

	Current liability	**Non-current liability**
A	Nil	$27,000
B	$6,000	$21,000
C	$21,000	$6,000
D	$27,000	Nil

374 What is the main purpose of a statement of financial position?

A To report the current value of the business

B To indicate if the business is trading profitably

C To report the assets and liabilities of the business

D To report the personal assets of the business owner

375 Billie's trial balance at 30 September 20X5 included the following balances:

Trade receivables	$75,943
Receivables allowance	$4,751

How should these balances be reported in Billie's statement of financial position as at 30 September 20X5?

A An asset of $71,192

B An asset of $75,943 and a liability of $4,751

C A liability of $71,192

D A liability of $75,943 and an asset of $4,751

376 Hansa's trial balance included a balance for drawings.

How should this balance be treated in the financial statements?

A As an expense in the statement of profit or loss

B As income in the statement of profit or loss

C As a reduction in capital

D As an increase in capital

377 When preparing the financial statements of a business, what entries should be made in a sole trader's capital account to record a loss for the year and drawings?

	Loss	Drawings
A	Debit	Debit
B	Credit	Credit
C	Debit	Debit
D	Debit	Credit

378 At 31 May 20X7 Sloka had a loan with an outstanding balance of $30,000. Sloka is required to repay $500 on the 10th day of each month.

How should the loan be reported in Sloka's statement of financial position at 31 May 20X7?

A As a current liability of $30,000

B As a current liability of $24,000 and a non-current liability of $6,000

C As a current liability of $6,000 and a non-current liability of $24,000

D As a non-current liability of $30,000

379 Whilst finalising the financial statements for the year ended 28 February 20X6, Baz noticed that a contra between the trade receivables' and trade payables' general ledger accounts which had been agreed with a customer who also supplied goods to the business had not yet been accounted for. The agreed amount of the contra was $2,500.

What are the accounting entries required to account for this contra?

A Debit discount received, and Credit trade receivables

B Debit trade payables, and Credit discount received

C Debit trade receivables, and Credit trade payables

D Debit trade payables, and Credit trade receivables

380 At 1 July 20X4 Ali was owed $30,468 by customers. During the year to 30 June 20X5, receipts from credit customers amounted to $105,382 and irrecoverable debts amounting to 2,500. Ali also needed to account for a contra between trade receivables' and trade payables' accounts amounting to $1,000. At 30 June 20X5 Ali was owed $27,532.

What was the value of Ali's credit sales for the year ended 30 June 20X5?

$

381 Maxi's trial balance at 30 November 20X2 included the following balances:

Machinery – at cost	$85,493
Machinery – accumulated depreciation	$7,514

How should these balances be reported in Maxi's statement of financial position as at 30 November 20X2?

A A liability of $77,979

B An asset of $85,493 and a liability of $7,514

C An asset of $77,979

D A liability of $85,493 and an asset of $7,514

382 Jiva's trial balance included an account balance for drawings made during the year.

How should this balance be treated in Jiva's final accounts?

A As an expense in the statement of profit or loss

B As income in the statement of profit or loss

C As a reduction in capital

D As an increase in capital

383 Sharrazinho Co recorded payments from customers of $5,000, recorded a bad debt expense of $1,500 and receivables at the end of the period was $22,500.

What is the missing figure for the period?

A Revenue $9,000

B Revenue $7,000

C Sales returns $6,000

D Sales returns $4,000

384 At 31 October 20X6 Gaz owed suppliers $13,856. During the year to 31 October 20X7, Gaz made payments to suppliers totalling $95,886, and at 31 October 20X7 owed suppliers $11,552.

What was the value of Gaz's credit purchases for the year ended 31 October 20X7?

$

385 In the year to 30 November 20X7, Shannon obtained a 25% mark up on all sales. Shannon's sales for the year totalled $120,600. Shannon's opening inventory was valued at $9,340 and the closing inventory was valued at $11,855.

What was the value of Shannon's purchases for the year to 30 November 20X7?

$

386 Pat does not keep a full set of accounting records, but the following information is available for the month of June 20X9:

	$
Accounts receivable, 1 June 20X9	800
Accounts receivable, 30 June 20X9	550
Credit sales	6,800
Cash received from credit customers	6,730
Irrecoverable written off	40
Allowance for receivables established 30 June 20X9	100

Assuming that there were no other transactions, what was the value of contras between the receivables' and payables' general ledger accounts for the month of June 20X9?

$

The following information relates to questions 387 to 392.

Taran has been in business as a freelance graphics designer for several years. Taran does not use the double-entry system to maintain detailed bookkeeping records. Instead, Taran analyses cash receipts and payments on a spreadsheet. Taran also keeps track of the amounts due from customers and owing to payables by means of a simple computerised record.

Taran's opening statement of financial position, as at 31 December 20X8, was as follows:

	Cost	**Accumulated depreciation**	**Carrying amount**
	$	$	$
Furniture	800	200	600
Computer	2,800	1,225	1,575
Printer	1,500	656	844
	5,100	2,081	3,019
Current assets			
Inventory of stationery and printer consumables		550	
Accounts receivable		800	
Bank		700	
		2,050	
Current liabilities – Accounts payable		70	
			1,980
			4,999
Long-term liabilities – Bank loan			2,400
Total assets less liabilities			2,599
Capital			2,599

Taran's analysis of cash receipts and payments for the year ended 31 December 20X9 was as follows:

	Receipts		**Payments**
	$		$
Received from clients	28,000	Drawings	24,000
Additional loan	2,000	Bank interest	400
		Suppliers of stationery and printer consumables	1,800
		Sundry expenses	600
	30,000		26,800

Taran's closing inventory of stationery cost $900. The accounts receivable totalled $1,300 and $200 was owed to suppliers. Furniture should be depreciated using 25% straight line and the computer and printer using 25% reducing balance.

Note: in the exam, all questions will be independent, and not based on a common scenario.

387 What was the value of Taran's sales for the year?

A $27,500

B $29,300

C $28,500

D $26,700

388 What was the cost of Taran's purchases figure for the year?

A $1,930

B $1,670

C $2,000

D $1,600

389 What was Taran's depreciation charge for the year?

A $755

B $805

C $1,225

D $1,275

390 What was Taran's capital at the year end?

A $3,714

B $4,400

C $8,114

D $8,314

391 What was Taran's profit for the year?

A $23,865

B $25,115

C $25,801

D $29,515

392 At 31 December 20X2, FCA Co had $100 in the cash till and it was discovered that some cash had been stolen.

At 1 January 20X2, there was $50 in the cash till and receivables were $2,000. Total sales for 20X2 were $230,000. Accounts receivable at 31 December 20X2 were $3,000. During 20X2, cheques banked from credit sales were $160,000 and cash sales of $50,000 have been banked.

How much cash was stolen during 20X2?

$

393 At 1 November 20X4 Bao owed $28,754 to suppliers. During the year Bao paid suppliers a total of $185,844. At 31 October 20X5 Bao owed $26,189.

What was the value of Bao's credit purchases in the year to 31 October 20X5?

$

394 During the year to 30 November 20X5 Jiang bought goods for resale at a cost of $75,550. Jiang's inventory at 1 December 20X4 was valued at $15,740. Jiang did not count inventory at 30 November 20X5, but knows that sales for the year ended 30 November 20X5 were $91,800. All sales were made at a mark-up of 20%.

Based on the information above, what was the value of Jiang's inventory at 30 November 20X5?

$

395 A business purchased goods on credit for $10,000; half the goods purchased were sold for cash at a mark-up of 120%. Sales commission of 5% was payable on this transaction. All takings were banked.

What was the net profit arising as a result of entering into these transactions?

$

396 During the year ended 30 April 20X8 Troy paid a total of $127,569 to suppliers. The opening and closing balances due to suppliers and the opening and closing inventory values were:

	Opening value	**Closing value**
Suppliers	$11,564	$12,826
Inventory	$5,288	$4,184

What was Troy's cost of sales for the year ended 30 April 20X8?

$

397 For the year ended 31 May 20X8 Les had sales of $600,000 and cost of sales of $480,000.

What are the correct figures for mark up and margin for the year ended 31 May 20X8?

	Mark up	**Margin**
A	25%	25%
B	25%	20%
C	20%	25%
D	20%	20%

398 For the year ended 31 August 20X2 Axl's sales totalled $850,000 and the cost of sales totalled $680,000.

What are the correct figures for Axl's mark up and margin for the year ended 31 August 20X2?

	Mark up	**Margin**
A	25%	25%
B	25%	20%
C	20%	25%
D	20%	20%

399 At 31 October 20X7 Tuli owed suppliers $24,786. During the year to 31 October 20X8, payments to suppliers totalled $104,886 and Tuli received prompt payment discounts of $750. Tuli also needed to account for a contra between the trade receivables and trade payables accounts amounting to $500. At 31 October 20X8 Tuli owed $23,552.

What was the cost of Tuli's credit purchases for the year ended 31 October 20X8?

$

400 For the year ended 31 July 20X3 Gopi's cost of sales totalled $250,000 and the gross profit was $50,000.

What are the correct figures for Gopi's mark up and margin for the year ended 31 July 20X3?

	Mark up	**Margin**
A	20%	16.7%
B	25%	20%
C	16.7%	20%
D	20%	20%

401 The following information is relevant to the calculation of the sales figure for Alpha, a sole trader who does not keep proper accounting records:

	$
Opening accounts receivable	29,100
Cash received from credit customers and paid into the bank	381,600
Expenses paid out of cash received from credit customers before banking	6,800
Irrecoverable debts written off	7,200
Refunds to credit customers	2,100
Contra with payables ledger	9,400
Cash sales	112,900
Closing accounts receivable	38,600

What figure should be included in Alpha's financial statements for revenue?

A $525,300

B $511,700

C $529,500

D $510,900

402 In the year ended 30 November 20X5, Lyn earned a 20% mark-up on cost on all sales made. Lyn's sales for the year totalled $240,600. Lyn's opening inventory was valued at $13,340 and the closing inventory was valued at $17,855.

What was the cost of Lyn's purchases for the year ended 30 November 20X5?

A $192,480

B $195,985

C $200,500

D $205,015

403 At 1 April 20X3 Yanlin was owed $22,785 by customers. During the year to 31 March 20X4, Yanlin's receipts from credit customers amounted to $95,723 and contras were agreed with credit customers who were also supplied with goods on credit of $3,750. Yanlin also wrote off an irrecoverable receivable of $350 during the year. At 31 March 20X4 Yanlin was owed $24,680 by credit customers.

What was the value of Yanlin's credit sales for the year ended 31 March 20X4?

A $101,718

B $97,968

C $97,618

D $101,368

404 At 1 July 20X7 Bo was owed $32,785 by customers. During the year to 30 June 20X8, Bo's receipts from credit customers amounted to $87,654. Bo agreed contras with other credit customers who were also suppliers to the business of $2,193 and received discounts of £3,219. Bo wrote off an irrecoverable receivable of $127 during the year. In August 20X7, $250 was received in respect of a receivable which had been written off in the previous accounting year which is not included within the total received from credit customers. At 31 March 20X4 Bo was owed $30,123 by credit customers.

What was the value of Bo's credit sales for the year ended 30 June 20X8?

A $84,220

B $87,312

C $87,562

D $87,062

405 Lou is a sole proprietor whose accounting records are incomplete. All the sales are cash sales and during the September 20X4 $34,200 was banked, including $3,250 from the sale of an old machine.

Also during September 20X4, Lou paid $3,500 wages in cash from the till and withdrew $1,500 as drawings. The cash in the till at 1 September 20X4 and at 30 September 20X4 was $250 and $350 respectively. There were no other payments during September 20X4.

What was the value of sales made in September 20X4?

A $36,450

B $39,300

C $36,050

D $36,120

406 Fran is a sole proprietor whose accounting records are incomplete. All the sales are cash sales and during May 20X1 $87,654 was banked, including $10,000 capital introduced.

During May 20X1, Fran paid $8,750 wages in cash from the till and withdrew $1,825 as drawings. During May 20X1, Fran also purchased a new laptop for business use, paying $750 cash. The cash in the till at 31 May 20X1 was $50 and at 1 May 20X1 was $70. There were no other payments during May 20X1.

What was the value of sales made in May 20X1?

A $88,979

B $88,209

C $98,959

D $88,959

407 Ali is a sole proprietor whose accounting records are incomplete. All the sales are cash sales and during August 20X5 $67,890 was banked.

During August 20X5, Ali withdrew $500 as drawing and paid $6,750 wages in cash from the till. The cash in the till at 1 August 20X5 was $100 and there was $200 in the cash till at 31 August 20X5. During August 20X5, Ali paid a repair bill of £350 in cash and paid for some purchases in cash, amounting to $3,728. In addition, Ali made a cash refund to a customer of $100 for return of goods. There were no other payments during August 20X5.

What was the value of sales made for the month of August 20X5?

A $79,318

B $79,418

C $79,068

D $79,518

408 Jital is a sole proprietor whose accounting records are incomplete. All sales are made for cash and during November 20X7 $26,543 was banked.

During November 20X7, Jital withdrew $1,750 for personal use and paid $3,750 wages in cash from the till. Jital also purchased new office furniture and equipment, paying $1,750 cash. The cash in the till at 30 November 20X7 was $50 and $70 at 1 November 20X7. There were no other payments made during November 20X7.

What was the value of Jital's cash sales for November 20X7?

$

409 For the year ended 30 September 20X5 Kahali's sales were $825,000. All of Kahali's sales were made at a mark-up of 25%. Kahali's opening inventory value was $12,800 and the closing inventory value was $14,700.

What was the cost of Kahali's purchases for the year ended 30 September 20X5?

$

410 At 1 April 20X5 Kinjal owed suppliers $21,876. During the year ended 31 March 20X6, Kinjal's payments to suppliers totalled $123,456 on which prompt payment discounts of $1,025 were received. Kinjal also needed to account for a contra between the trade receivables and trade payables accounts amounting to $2,500. At 31 October 20X8 Kinjal owed $19,998.

What was the cost of Kinjal's credit purchases for the year ended 31 March 20X6?

$

411 During the year ended 31 December 20X9 Folland Co's revenue totalled $3,000,000 and its accounts receivable amounted to 4% of sales revenue for the year. At 31 December 20X9, Folland Co wishes have an allowance for receivables of $3,600, and discovered that this allowance is 25% higher than it was at 31 December 20X8. During the year ended 31 December 20X9, specific irrecoverable amounts of $3,200 were written off and irrecoverable debts (written off three years previously) of $150 were recovered.

What was the net charge to profit or loss for irrecoverable debts and allowance for receivables for the year ended 31 December 20X9?

A $3,450

B $3,770

C $3,920

D $3,600

412 At the beginning of its accounting period a business had accounts receivable of $13,720 after deducting an allowance for receivables of $630. At the year end, accounts receivable before any allowances amounted to $17,500 and an allowance for receivables of $525 was required.

What is the charge or credit to profit or loss in relation to the change in the allowance for receivables for the year?

A $525 Debit to profit or loss

B $735 Debit to profit or loss

C $105 Credit to profit or loss

D $420 Credit to profit or loss

413 At 30 September 20X4, Z Co had an allowance for receivables of $37,000. During the year ended 30 September 20X5 Z Co wrote off debts totalling $18,000, and at 30 September 20X5 it was decided that the allowance for receivables should be $20,000.

What was included in profit or loss for irrecoverable debts and allowance for receivables?

A $35,000 debit

B $1,000 debit

C $38,000 debit

D $1,000 credit

414 At 30 November 20X6 the balance on Umang's receivables ledger was $37,890. At that date, Umang decided to write off balances totalling $1,570 and calculated that the allowance for receivables should be increased from $250 to $1,158 at 30 November 20X6.

What was the net receivables balance that was reported in Umang's statement of financial position at 30 November 20X6?

A $35,412

B $35,162

C $36,320

D $36,070

415 **What adjustments is required write off an irrecoverable balance due from a customer?**

A Debit Revenue, and Credit Receivables expense

B Debit Irrecoverable debts, and Credit Revenue

C Debit Irrecoverable debts, and Credit Trade receivables

D Debit Trade receivables, and Credit Irrecoverable debt

416 During the year ended 30 April 20X6 Petra's sales were $182,000. All of Petra's sales were made at a mark-up of 30%. Petra's opening inventory value was $11,800 and closing inventory value was $9,700.

What was the cost of Petra's purchases in the year ended 30 April 20X6?

$

417 During June 20X8 Laurie bought goods for $12,000. Laurie paid $11,000 of this by cheque immediately and agreed a 30 day credit period for the balance. Laurie intends to buy more goods at a cost of $13,000 in July 20X8.

What liability should be reported for Laurie's payables at 30 June 20X8?

$

PARTNERSHIPS

418 Which of the following statements relating to accounting for a partnership is true?

A The partners' capital accounts reflect each partner's share of profit from the appropriation account.

B If a partner makes a loan to the partnership, this is classified as an increase in the capital account of that partner.

C The capital account of each partner is normally fixed and will change when a partner introduces additional capital into the business or retires from the partnership.

D The capital account of each partner is debited with drawings made during the accounting year.

419 Which of the following statements relating to accounting for a partnership is true?

A The respective share of profit from the appropriation account is recorded in the current account of each partner.

B If a partner has a salary from the partnership, this is accounted for as an expense in the statement of profit or loss.

C If interest is earned on capital account balances, the interest earned is credited to the capital account of each partner.

D The capital account balances of each partner must have identical account balances.

420 Which of the following statements provides the definition of a partnership?

A A maximum of three people in business together

B Persons in business together with the intention of sharing profits and losses

C Two work colleagues who are employed by the same business

D Two persons who each have their own business as a sole proprietor

421 What is the purpose of a partnership agreement?

A It is a legal requirement for all partnerships to have a partnership agreement.

B It enables customers to understand how the partnership operates.

C It is a contract between the partners that sets out their rights and responsibilities to each other.

D It is a contract between the partners that sets out the profit and loss sharing arrangements between the partners.

422 Which of the following items would not normally be included within a partnership agreement?

A The names of the partners

B The arrangements for sharing residual profits and losses between the partners

C The name and business location of the partnership

D The names of the principal customers and suppliers of the business

---

The following information relates to questions 423 and 424.

Viv and Bao are in partnership, sharing profits and losses in a ratio of 3:2. The business maintains current accounts and fixed capital accounts for the partners. In the last year, the profit before appropriations was $27,800. Bao is entitled to an annual salary of $3,800.

During the year Viv and Bao made cash drawings of $12,000 each.

Note: in the exam, all questions will be independent, and not based on a common scenario.

---

423 What is Viv's share of the profit?

A $2,280

B $9,600

C $14,400

D $16,680

424 The correct entry for the partners' drawings has been made in the cash account.

What entry is needed to complete the posting for the partners' drawings?

A A debit entry in the partners' capital accounts

B A credit entry in the partners' capital accounts

C A debit entry in the partners' current accounts

D A credit entry in the partners' current accounts

425 Ali and Dai are in partnership, sharing profits and losses in the ratio 3:2. Under the terms of the partnership agreement, Dai is entitled to a salary of $8,000. The partnership statement of profit or loss for the year to 30 November 20X4 reported a profit of $16,000.

What is Ali's share of the profit?

$

426 Alex and Kim are in partnership. In the year to 31 October 20X6, Alex's drawings were $18,000 and the following entries have been made in the partnership appropriation account for Alex:

	$
Salary	6,500
Interest on drawings	1,800
Share of profit	12,750

At 1 November 20X5, the balance on Alex's current account was $24,800 (credit).

What was the balance on Alex's current account at 31 October 20X6?

$

The following information relates to questions 427 to 429

Hub Design has three partners: M, J and A. The three share profits equally after interest on capital at 5% and J's partnership salary of $8,000. The partners' account balances are shown below:

	M	**J**	**A**	**Total**
Capital	$20,000	$15,000	$40,000	$75,000
Current	$100,000	$80,000	$110,000	$290,000
Drawings	$30,000	$35,000	$40,000	$105,000

No interest is paid on current account balances.

The net profit for the year ended 31 December 20X6 is $170,000.

Note: in the exam, all questions will be independent, and not based on a common scenario.

---

427 **What will the statement of financial position as at 31 December 20X6 show as the total for owners' equity?**

$

428 **What will each partner receive as a share of residual profit?**

$

429 **What total profit will J receive for the year ended 31 December 20X6?**

$

430 Jo and Sam are in partnership sharing profits and losses in the ratio 3:4. The statement of profit or loss for the year to 31 May 20X6 reported a net profit of $30,709. Jo is entitled to a salary of $14,000 per annum.

What was Sam's share of the profit for the year to 31 May 20X6?

$

431 Kranti and Lazim are in partnership sharing profits and losses in the ratio 2:3. The statement of profit or loss for the year ended 31 August 20X3 reported a net profit of $73,540. Kranti is entitled to a salary of $18,000 per annum.

What was Kranti's total share of the profit for the year to 31 August 20X3?

A $40,216

B $22,216

C $33,324

D $51,324

432 Manvi and Nartan are in partnership sharing profits and losses in the ratio 6:4. The statement of profit or loss for the year ended 31 January 20X8 reported a net profit of $24,680. Nartan is entitled to a salary of $5,000 per annum.

What was Nartan's total share of the profit for the year to 31 January 20X8?

A $11,808

B $12,872

C $7,872

D $9,872

433 Pahal and Parul are in partnership sharing profits and losses in the ratio 7:3. The statement of profit or loss for the year ended 31 July 20X7 reported a net profit of $52,900. Pahal is entitled to an annual salary of $14,000 and Parul is entitled to an annual salary of $6,000.

What was Parul's total share of the profit for the year ended 31 July 20X7?

$

434 Pavi and Razz and are in partnership sharing profits and losses in the ratio 90:10. The statement of profit or loss for the year ended 28 February 20X4 reported a net profit of $36,600. Razz is entitled to an annual salary of $12,500.

What is Razz's total share of the profit for the year to 28 February 20X4?

A $3,660

B $34,190

C $21,690

D $14,910

The following information relates to questions 435 and 436.

Reema and Rimple are in partnership sharing profits and losses in the ratio 3:5. Reema is also entitled to a salary of $5,000. At 1 June 20X5, the business had the following credit balances on the capital and current accounts of the partners:

	Reema	Rimple
Capital	$80,000	$60,000
Current	$21,735	$14,876

During the year ended 30 June 20X6, Reema and Rimple made drawings of $27,500 and $26,500 respectively. For the year ended 31 May 20X6, the statement of profit or loss for the partnership disclosed a profit of $60,000.

Note: in the exam, all questions will be independent, and not based on a common scenario.

435 What is the balance on Rimple's current account at 31 May 20X6?

A $19,860

B $22,751

C $7,875

D $25,876

436 What is the balance on Reema's current account at 31 May 20X6?

$

437 Kia and Ali are in partnership sharing profits and losses in the ratio 2:3. Kia is entitled to a salary of $3,500 and Ali is entitled to a salary of $2,500. At 1 September 20X6, the business had the following credit balances on the partners' capital and current accounts:

	Kia	Ali
Capital	$80,000	$60,000
Current	$14,769	$13,748

During the year ended 31 August 20X7, Kia and Ali made drawings of $38,775 and $43,915 respectively. For the year ended 31 August 20X7, the statement of profit or loss for the partnership disclosed a profit of $80,000.

What was the balance on Kia's current account at 31 August 20X7?

$

The following information relates to questions 438 to 442.

Three's A Crowd has three partners: Sai, Taran and Veda. The three partners share profits equally after interest on capital at 5% and Sai's partnership salary of $12,500. The partners' account balances at 31 July 20X4 are shown below:

	Sai	Taran	Veda
Capital	$20,000	$20,000	$10,000
Current	$7,000	$5,250	$8,375
Drawings	$13,750	$11,250	$9,500

No interest is paid on current account balances.

The net profit for the year ended 31 July 20X4 was $150,000.

Note: in the exam, all questions will be independent, and not based on a common scenario.

438 What will the statement of financial position as at 31 July 20X4 show as the total for owners' equity?

A $186,125

B $255,125

C $36,125

D $165,500

439 What will each partner receive as a share of residual profit?

A $50,000

B $45,000

C $49,167

D $45,833

440 What total profit will Sai receive for the year ended 31 July 20X4?

A $46,000

B $57,500

C $58,500

D $60,000

441 What will Sai's current account balance be after accounting for the profit share for the year ended 31 July 20X4?

A $50,750

B $65,500

C $44,750

D $51,750

442 What will the total of the partners' current account balances at 31 July 20X4?

A $136,125

B $170,625

C $205,125

D $115,500

The following information relates to questions 443 and 444.

'Three's Two Much' has three partners: Tulli, Vishva and Sam. The three partners share profits and losses equally after interest on capital at 10% and partnership salaries of $8,000 for Tulli, $10,000 for Vishva and $12,000 for Sam. The partners' account balances at 31 July 20X4 are shown below:

	Tulli	**Vishva**	**Sam**
Capital	$50,000	$50,000	$20,000
Current	$7,000	$5,250	$8,375
Drawings	$13,750	$11,250	$9,500

No interest is paid on current account balances.

The net profit for the year ended 31 July 20X4 was $45,000.

Note: in the exam, all questions will be independent, and not based on a common scenario.

443 What will each partner receive as a share of residual profit or loss for the year?

A $1,000 profit

B $15,000 profit

C $1,000 loss

D $5,000 profit

444 What total profit share will Tulli receive for the year ended 31 July 20X4?

A $7,000

B $12,000

C $13,000

D $14,000

445 How should each of the following be accounted for?

	Business expense	**Profit appropriation**
Salary paid to an employee		
Salary paid to a partner		

446 Which of the following items would normally be accounted for in the capital account of a partner?

A Cash introduced upon joining a partnership

B Cash drawings from the business for personal use

C Their share of profit or loss for the year

D Goods withdrawn from the business for personal use

447 Which of the following items would not be accounted for in the current account of a partner?

A The share of residual profit or loss for the year that the partner is entitled to

B Accounting for goodwill upon retirement of a partner

C Interest on capital

D Interest charged on overdrawn current account balances

The following information relates to questions 448 to 450.

Triple Stripe has three partners: Hong, Lian and Zac. The three partners share profits in the ratio 40:40:20 after interest on capital accounts at 4% and Lian's partnership salary of $7,500. The partners' account balances are shown below:

	Hong	**Lian**	**Zak**	**Total**
Capital account at 1 August 20X2	$32,000	$28,000	$20,000	$80,000
Current account at 1 August 20X2	$51,000	$45,000	$25,000	$121,000
Drawings for the year ended 31 July 20X3	$27,000	$32,000	$12,000	$71,000

No interest is paid on current account balances or charged on overdrawn current account balances. The net profit for the year ended 31 July 20X3 was $180,000.

Note: in the exam, all questions will be independent, and not based on a common scenario.

448 What was the total for owners' equity in the statement of financial position as at 31 July 20X3?

A $80,000

B $121,000

C $131,000

D $310,000

449 What did Hong receive as a share of residual profit for the year ended 31 July 20X3?

A $33,860

B $67,720

C $69,000

D $72,000

450 What total profit share did Lian receive for the year ended 31 July 20X3?

A $72,000

B $67,720

C $76,340

D $75,220

451 When accounting for goodwill upon admission of a partner, and having accounted for goodwill as an asset, what accounting entries are then required to remove goodwill from the partnership accounting records?

	Debit	Credit
Partners' capital accounts		
Goodwill		

452 Nuwa and Suyin are in partnership and share profits and losses equally. On 1 January 20X8, Maz is admitted to the partnership and it was agreed that, from that date, profits and losses would be shared equally between the three partners. Goodwill was valued at $60,000. Nuwa and Suyin had the following credit balances on their capital and current accounts at 1 January 20X8:

	Nuwa	Suyin
Capital	$60,000	$60,000
Current	$15,000	$10,000

A goodwill account is not maintained in the books of the partnership.

How much is Maz required to contribute to have a capital account credit balance of $10,000 immediately after joining the partnership?

A $10,000

B $20,000

C $30,000

D $60,000

453 Ali, Chris and Mai are in partnership and share profits and losses equally. Ali decided to retire with effect from 31 December 20X7 and it was agreed that Ali would withdraw cash for the full amount due on the capital and current account balances at that date. Goodwill was valued at $60,000 at 31 December 20X7. Chris and Mai will continue in partnership and will share profits and losses in the ratio 30:20 Ali, Chris and Mai had the following credit balances on their capital and current accounts at 31 December 20X7 prior to accounting for Ali's retirement:

	Ali	Chris	Mai
Capital	$60,000	$60,000	40,000
Current	$15,000	$10,000	5,000

A goodwill account is not maintained in the books of the partnership.

How much will Ali withdraw from the partnership at the date of retirement?

A $55,000

B $95,000

C $65,000

D $25,000

454 Jo and Terri are in partnership and share profits and losses in the proportion 4:2. On 1 January 20X8, Maz was admitted to the partnership and it was agreed that, from that date, profits and losses would be shared equally between the three partners. Goodwill was valued at $75,000. Jo and Terri had the following credit balances on their capital and current accounts at 1 January 20X8:

	Jo	**Terri**
Capital	$50,000	$50,000
Current	$8,000	$7,000

A goodwill account is not maintained in the books of the partnership.

How much is required to be contributed if Maz is to have a capital account credit balance of $5,000 immediately after joining the partnership?

A $10,000

B $20,000

C $30,000

D $60,000

455 Vic, Em and Lou are in partnership and share profits and losses equally. Vic decided to retire with effect from 31 December 20X6 and it was agreed that Vic would withdraw cash for the full amount due to the capital and current account balances at that date. Goodwill was valued at $90,000 at 31 December 20X6. Em and Lou will continue in partnership and will share profits and losses in the ratio 5:3. Vica, Em and Lou had the following credit balances on their capital and current accounts at 31 December 20X6 immediately prior to accounting for Victoria's retirement:

	Vic	**Em**	**Lou**
Capital	$25,000	$25,000	35,000
Current	$5,000	$10,000	2,000

A goodwill account is not maintained in the books of the partnership.

How much will Vic withdraw from the partnership at the date of retirement?

A $55,000

B $30,000

C $55,000

D $60,000

Section 3

ANSWERS TO REVISION QUESTIONS – SECTION A

ACCOUNTING PRINCIPLES AND CONCEPTS

1 Accounting standards improve financial accounting by providing the basis for generally accepted accounting practice (GAAP). This arises because standards:

- reduce variations in accounting practice by specifying how particular issues should be treated
- provide a reference point when choosing between alternative accounting treatments
- encourage debate, which (generally) leads to a commonly accepted practice
- whilst providing a framework, allow a degree of flexibility which may be difficult to achieve by adopting a legislative approach.

2 The going concern concept states that, unless there is evidence to the contrary, accounts should be prepared on the assumption that the business will continue for the foreseeable future, and that it will not be liquidated or significantly reduced in scale. This means that the assets will not be valued at their 'break-up' (individual market) value.

3 **Relevance**

Information is relevant if:

- it will influence the economic decisions of users; and
- it is provided on a timely basis.

Faithful Representation

If information is to represent faithfully the transactions and other events that it purports to represent, they must be accounted for and presented in accordance with their substance and economic reality and not merely their legal form.

To be a perfectly faithful representation, financial information would possess the following characteristics:

(a) it is complete

(b) it is free from deliberate or systematic bias (i.e. it is neutral)

(c) it is free from material error

Enhancing characteristics:

Comparability

This means that information can be compared either with previous periods for the same business or with other businesses.

This is usually achieved by the consistent application of accounting policies from one period to the next, and by disclosure of those policies.

Verifiability

Verifiability is a quality of information that means the information is supportable, i.e. it can be verified.

Verification can be direct or indirect. Direct verification means verifying an amount or other representation through direct observation i.e. counting cash. Indirect verification means checking the inputs to a model, formula or other technique and recalculating the outputs using the same methodology i.e. recalculating inventory amounts using the same cost flow assumption such as first in, first out method.

Timeliness

Timeliness means having information available to decision makers in time to be capable of influencing their decisions. Generally, the older the information is the less useful it becomes.

Understandability

This term means that financial information should be capable of being understood. It should be noted that this test is applied in the context of the users having a reasonable knowledge of accounting and business.

Effectively this means that the formats and disclosures laid down by the regulatory framework should be considered to be minimum requirements, and additional information should be provided as necessary.

4 The business entity concept states that, no matter what the legal status of the business, in accounting terms we always keep the business and the owner separate.

This means that, when recording transactions, we are only concerned with how the business is affected. For example, if the owner introduces capital, we are not concerned with the source of the capital and, apart from increasing the owner's capital balance, we do not record how the owner is affected by the transaction.

5 Transactions are recorded by both a debit entry and a credit entry (also referred to as 'double entry') as this reflects the effects of the transaction on the entity. Every transaction affects the entity in two ways. This is usually referred to as the 'dual aspect'. The two effects mean that the accounting equation (Assets – Liabilities = Capital) will apply consistently to the entity.

For example, if expenses are paid in cash, the entity is affected by an increase in the expense and a reduction in cash. The increase in the expense will cause a reduction in profit, and therefore capital. Thus both assets and capital have reduced, and the accounting equation will continue to apply.

BASIC BOOKKEEPING

6 In the IASB's *Conceptual framework for financial reporting*, an asset is defined as 'a present economic resource controlled by the entity as a result of past events'. An asset may be classified as either a current or non-current asset in the statement of financial position.

A liability is defined as 'a present obligation of the entity to transfer an economic resource as a result of past events'. An economic resource is 'a right that has the potential to produce economic benefits'. A liability may be classified as either a current or non-current liabil9ity in the statement of financial position.

An example of a current asset is an amount owed to a business entity for goods sold on credit to a customer. An example of a non-current asset is property, plant and equipment owned and used by a business.

The balance due for repayment on a long-term loan is an example of a non-current liability. A bank overdraft is an example of a current liability.

7 When goods are purchased on credit, both assets and liabilities will increase by the same amount, but capital will be unaffected. This is because:

- the cost of the items purchased will be included in the inventory of the business
- the liability to suppliers will rise by the same amount; and
- as no profit has been earned, and no expense has been incurred, capital will remain unchanged.

8 When a credit customer is not expected to take advantage of early settlement discount offered, the settlement discount is not deducted in arriving at the invoice price. If the customer, as expected, does not pay early, the amount subsequently paid should match the invoice and receivable previously recorded.

If, however, the customer does pay within the time period to be eligible for the settlement discount, both revenue and the receivable is reduced to match with the cash received. The sales ledger account of the individual customer should also be updated.

9 When a credit customer is expected to take advantage of early settlement discount offered, the settlement discount is deducted in arriving at the invoice price. In this situation, settlement discount is treated in the same way as trade discount and excluded from the invoice price. If the customer, as expected, does pay early, the amount subsequently paid should match the invoice and receivable previously recorded.

If, however, the customer pays outside of time to be eligible for the settlement discount, the full amount is receivable and the amount received in excess of the revenue and receivable previously recorded is accounted for as additional revenue.

NON-CURRENT ASSETS AND DEPRECIATION

10 There are several reasons for a difference between the assets in the non-current asset register and those physically present in the business. For example, the non-current asset register may not have been updated to reflect the purchase of a new asset or the disposal of an old asset. In addition, an error may have been made when an entry was originally made in the records.

11 The factors to consider would be the original cost less depreciation to date, compared with the proceeds from the sale.

12

	Depreciation charge	**Cost/carrying value**
	$	$
Original cost		15,000
Year 1	15,000 × 25% = 3,750	15,000 – 3,750 = 11,250
year 2	11,250 × 25% = 2,813	11,250 – 2,813 = 8,437
year 3	8,437 × 25% = 2,109	8,437 – 2,109 = 6,328
Year 4	6,328 × 25% = 1,582	6,328 – 1,582 = 4,746
Year 5	4,746 × 25% = 1,187	4,746 – 1,187 = 3,559

RECONCILIATIONS AND ERRORS

13 This is an error of principle – an asset, which is a capital or asset expenditure, has been charged to revenue expenditure account. It should be classified as asset expenditure and included as part of non-current assets. The chairs will be used for over several years and should be capitalised and depreciated over their useful economic life to the business.

14 The reasons for disagreement between the bank general ledger account balance and bank statement balances can be: timing differences for unpresented cheques and automated payments and outstanding lodgements, together with standing order and BACS receipts and payments, and bank charges and interest.

ADJUSTMENTS TO THE TRIAL BALANCE

15 The main purpose of a trial balance is to ensure that debit balances and credit balances are equal. This provides a basic check on the accuracy of the postings.

16 An irrecoverable debt is a debt considered to be bad and unlikely to be paid by the customer. Irrecoverable debts are written off as an expense in the statement of profit or loss. The relevant receivables account is reduced accordingly.

An allowance for receivables is made for debts where there is some basis for uncertainty that they will be fully recovered. The business makes an allowance for receivables, based upon objective evidence available. Examples of evidence that may support the creation of an allowance for receivables include: amount due disputed by the customer or goods identified as faulty or not received or the amount is overdue for payment. Any increase or decrease in the allowance is credited or debited to the statement of profit or loss. The full amount of the allowance is deducted from the figure of receivables shown in the statement of financial position. The accounts of the individual receivables remain unaffected.

17 They would be valued at $180 – their NRV (net realisable value) complying with the prudence concept.

18 Accruals and prepayments include provisions and adjustments covered by the matching or accruals concept.

The concept ensures that income and costs are matched to the trading period in which they were generated or incurred and not when the income is received or the expenditure paid.

FINAL ACCOUNTS

19 (i) The statement of profit or loss shows the financial performance of a business for a period of time. It reports the revenue earned and expenses incurred in the period.

(ii) The statement of financial position reports the overall financial position of a business at a particular date, by reporting the assets, liabilities and capital balances.

20 Items include:

- drawings
- interest on drawings
- salary
- share of profit.

A closing credit balance represents a partner's accumulated share of retained profits.

21 A partnership agreement typically includes the following issues:

- amount of capital to be introduced by partners
- how profits are to be shared between partners (this may be by reference to interest on capital, notional salaries and a residual profit share)
- drawings by partners and interest thereon
- agreed business activities, along with any specifically excluded activities
- procedure for resolving disputes
- arrangements for dissolution of the partnership on the death or retirement of partners.

22 The five steps to recognise revenue in the financial statements are as follows:

- identify the contract with a customer
- identify the performance obligations of the contract
- determine the transaction price
- allocate the transaction price to the performance obligations in the contract
- recognise revenue when (or as) the entity satisfies a performance obligation.

23 The current account of a partner will normally reflect the following items:

- interest earned on capital accounts, if agreed between the partners
- interest charged on overdrawn current accounts, if agreed between the partners
- salary awarded, if agreed between the partners
- the share of residual profit, based upon the profit-sharing ratio
- drawings made during the accounting period.

The capital account will record the capital introduced when the partner joined the partnership. It will normally remain unchanged, unless additional capital is introduced into the business, or the partner retires from the partnership.

Section 4

ANSWERS TO OBJECTIVE TEST QUESTIONS – SECTION B

ACCOUNTING PRINCIPLES AND CONCEPTS

1 B

Financial statements should disclose all material items that are likely to affect the decisions of users.

2 D

Consistent accounting treatment should be applied to transactions both within an accounting period, and from one accounting period to another.

3 C

4

	Statement of profit or loss	**Statement of financial position**
Expenses	Correct	
Equity		Correct

5 B

6 A

7 B

Purchases should be recorded when the transaction takes place, which in this case is on receipt of the items. If a business waits until receipt of the invoice to record a purchase, there could be an opportunity for 'window dressing' of the accounts at the end of the year, by asking suppliers not to send in invoices until later.

8 D

Financial records should be maintained to enable the business owner to meet a range of uses, for both internal decision-making and to provide to external interested parties.

9 D

Providing information to the general public considers the external perspective of maintaining financial records.

10 B

Enabling the proprietor to make investment decisions considers the internal perspective of maintaining financial records.

11 D

12

	Selected answer
To reclaim sales tax	Correct
To record how much is owed to the customer	
To identify the goods bought	Correct
To record how much is owed from the customer	

13 C

14 C

15 B

The **Framework** identifies two fundamental qualitative characteristics, relevance and faithful representation, together with a further four enhancing qualitative characteristics – comparability, verifiability, timeliness and understandability.

16

	Fundamental qualitative characteristic	**Enhancing qualitative characteristic**
Understandability		Correct
Faithful representation	Correct	

17

	Selected answer
Going concern	
Comparability	Correct
Timeliness	Correct
Relevance	

18

	Selected answer
Verifiability	Correct
Materiality	
Historical cost	
Understandability	Correct

19

	Selected answer
Relevance	Correct
Reliability	
Faithful representation	Correct
Verifiability	

20 **B**

21 **D**

22 **C**

23 **C**

24 **A**

25 **D**

PRINCIPLES AND PROCESSES OF BASIC BOOKKEEPING

26 **C**

27 **A**

28 **D**

29 **C**

30 **B**

31 **A**

32 **C**

33 D

34 A

35 C

Chocolates not yet sold to customers are the inventory of T's Sweets Co. Inventory is classed as a current asset. The head office is an item of property, plant and equipment, which would be considered a non-current asset. Overdrafts and trade payables are current liabilities, not current assets.

36 B

The receipt from a credit customer would lead to an increase in cash at bank and a reduction in receivables. The net position is that total assets have not changes. Cash injected into the business would increase assets (cash ant bank) and also the owner's capital account. Settlement of the amount due to the supplier would reduce the cash at bank balance. The purchase of a machine would increase assets.

37 B

An asset is 'a present economic resource controlled by an entity as a result of past events'.

38 D

39 B

40 C

41 D

42 D

43 A

44 C

45

	Selected answer
Statement of financial position	Correct
Bank statement	
Statement of profit or loss	Correct
Supplier statement	

46 D

47 B

48

	True/False
With a cloud accounting system, an accountant or auditor can be granted remote access to data and information they require	True
With a cloud accounting system all employees are granted access to all data and information in the system	False

An accountant or auditor can be granted access to the cloud accounting system to enable them to prepare information and documents, such as sales tax returns or the annual financial statements. Not all employees will have access to all parts of the system. For example, access to payroll data and information is likely to be restricted to staff having responsibility for processing and management of the payroll.

49 A

50 C

51 D

The trial balance does not guarantee that all transactions have been correctly posted to the correct general ledger accounts, or that there will not be any errors contained within those ledger accounts. It will confirm, however, that an equal value of debits and credits have been posted into the general ledger accounts.

52 B

The trial balance may contain errors within individual general ledger accounts. It does not confirm the profit or loss for the accounting period. The proprietor's capital account balance at the end of the accounting period will be confirmed when the final accounts are produced.

53 B

54

	Selected answers
Petty cash	Correct
Bank loan	
Receivables	Correct
Proprietor's capital account	

55 B

The statement of profit or loss confirms whether an entity made a profit or loss for the trading period. The trial balance and general ledger accounts may still contain errors if transactions have been omitted or duplicated, or if transactions have been posted to the wrong ledger account(s).

56 C

THE PREPARATION OF JOURNALS AND LEDGER ACCOUNTS

57 D

The receivables account is debited with the gross amount owed, including sales tax. The sales account is credited with the net sale value (i.e. excluding sales tax). The tax on sales, which is payable to the government, is a liability and credited to a sales tax account.

58 C

Returns inwards are sales returns from customers. They can be thought of as 'negative sales' or 'negative income', so we debit a returns inwards account. The returns reduce the amount owed by credit customers, so we credit the receivables account (reducing an asset = credit entry).

59 A

Returns outwards are returns made to suppliers, perhaps because goods received were damaged i.e. they are 'negative purchases'. The liability to the supplier must be reduced and the returns outwards account is credited. At the end of the year, the total of returns outwards will be offset against the purchases expense to reduce the net cost of purchases.

60 C

Trade discount should not be recognised in the general ledger accounts. Settlement discount relating to the early payment of amounts due to suppliers is discount received.

61 C

This is a transaction that records an increase in non-current assets (motor vehicle) and an increase in capital.

62 D

Before the debt was written-off it was recognised in receivables (with or without a related allowance for doubtful debts). To remove the debt receivables will be credited and a charge for irrecoverable debts will be recognised in profit or loss.

63 D

Cash sales do not affect receivables. Discounts received affect payables, not receivables.

The allowance for receivables does not affect receivables, but specific irrecoverable debts written off do affect receivables.

Receivables

	$		$
Opening balance b/d	42,750	Contra with payables	18,750
Sales (credit sales)	362,750	Irrecoverable debts w/off	8,640
		Bank (balancing figure)	333,785
		Closing balance c/d	44,325
	405,500		405,500
Balance b/d	44,325		

64 D

65 B

66 C

67 D

68 A

69 $12,231 credit

Purchases

	$		$
Purchases – Jan	4,700	Journal 25	1,327
Purchases – Feb	3,387		
Purchases – Mar	5,471	**Balance carried down**	12,231
	13,558		13,558
Balance brought down	12,231		

70 $35,139 credit

Sales

	$		$
Journal	854	Balance brought forward	18,471
		Sales – Jun	4,200
		Sales – Jul	5,387
Balance carried down	35,139	Sales – Aug	7,935
	35,993		35,993
		Balance brought down	**35,139**

RECORDING TRANSACTIONS AND EVENTS

71 D

72 C

73 D

74 B

75 A

76 D

77 A

78 B

79 C

80 A

81 D

82 A

83 B

The balances provided in the question are correctly classified as follows:

	$	
Machinery at cost	85,800	non-current asset
Accumulated depreciation on machinery	21,750	reduction in non-current asset
Trade receivables	42,650	current asset
Receivables allowance	1,570	reduction in current asset
Bank overdraft	6,470	current liability
Inventory at 1 November 20X6	21,650	charge in profit or loss

The inventory at 31 October 20X7 of $22,300 is also a current asset.

The total value of current assets is: $63,380 ($42,650 – $1,570 + $22,300)

84 $4,273

Opening accrual	$297	Credit
Payments made	$4,570	Debit
Balance at 31 October 20X7	$4,273	Debit

NB: There is no closing accrual or prepayment as the invoices cover the period up to the end of the financial year.

85 D

86 C

	$	
Receivables balance	78,600	
Less Irrecoverable amount	(600)	
Revised balance	78,000	
Allowance at 1.5% =	1,170	
Existing allowance	1,200	
Reduction	30	i.e. credit to profit or loss

87 D

The accounting equation is Assets = Capital + Liabilities. Therefore, to have capital of $10,000, the accounting equation must be:

Assets ($14,000) = Capital ($10,000) + Liabilities ($4,000)

88 D

89 $1,500

	$
Closing capital	4,500
Opening capital	(10,000)
Decrease in net assets	(5,500)
Drawings: profit taken out	8,000
Capital introduced	(4,000)
Loss for the year	(1,500)

90 $38,020

Current liabilities are:	$
Trade payables	32,165
Bank overdraft	5,855
	38,020

91 C

The purchase return reduces the amount owed to the supplier by $800 plus sales tax.

$800 + (10% × $800) = $880.00

92 $3,800

Sales tax account

	$		$
Payables/bank (input sales tax)	6,000	Balance b/d	3,400
Bank	2,600	Receivables/bank (output sales tax)	9,000
Balance c/d	3,800		
	12,400		12,400
		Balance b/d	3,800

Tax on sales (outputs) = 15% × $60,000 = $9,000

Tax on purchases (inputs) = (15/115) × $46,000 = $6,000

93 $3,045

The only item of current liabilities in the list is 'payables', which are $3,045.

94 $3,000

Non-current assets in the list are motor vehicles and fixtures and fittings, which are:

$2,400 + 600 = $3,000

95 $2,732

$18,955 – 11,334 – 2,447 – 664 – 456 – 120 –146 – 276 – 665 – 115 = $2,732

96 A

Closing inventory is debited to the inventory account, and is the opening balance for the start of the next accounting period. Closing inventory also reduces the cost of sales, and so is credited to the statement of profit or loss.

97 D

The statement of financial position is a list of balances, not a general ledger account. Therefore no double entry is required.

98 B

The series of transactions might be recorded as follows:

Original purchase: Debit Purchases, and Credit accounts payable

On payment: Debit Accounts payable and Credit Bank

Therefore, on cancellation of the cheque: Debit Bank, and Accounts payable

99 B

A bank overdraft represents money owed to the bank. Legally it is repayable on demand is classified as a current liability.

100 $74,890

	$
Opening capital	68,920
Add profit for the year	22,860
Less drawings in the year	(16,890)
Closing capital	74,890

101 C

The loan is a liability; this is shown as a credit in the statement of financial position.

The cash in hand is an asset; this is shown as a debit in the statement of financial position.

Assets and liabilities must be shown separately; they can only be netted-off if there is a legal right of set-off.

102 $19,000

Sales of $150,000 at a margin of 20% = a gross profit of $30,000.

Therefore cost of sales is $120,000 ($150,000 – $30,000)

Cost of sales =	Opening inventory +	Purchases –	Closing inventory, thus:
$120,000 =	$12,500 +	$126,500 –	$19,000 (balancing figure)

103 $34,050

Increase in capital is $8,286. This represents profit less drawings.

Therefore, profit is $8,286 + $25,764 = $34,050.

104 C

Assets will be increased by the purchase of the computer, and liabilities will be increased by the new loan.

105 C

Property repairs are an expense. As this has been incorrectly treated as asset expenditure, expenses are understated (and therefore profit is overstated) and assets are overstated.

106 $40,191

Capital	=		$
		Non-current assets	33,750
	+	Inventory	4,845
	+	Receivables	11,248
	–	Payables	(9,633)
	–	Bank overdraft	(539)
	+	Prepayment	520
			40,191

107 D

108 $17,649

	$
Inventory	5,754
Receivables	11,745
Cash at bank	150
	17,649

109 A

Invoices	$4,728	Dr
Opening accrual	$353	Cr
Closing balance	$4,375	Dr

110 C

Balance per ledger	$31,554	Cr
Discount	$53	Dr
Invoice	$622	Cr
Corrected balance	$32,123	

111 D

112 D

113 $72,185

	$
Inventory	25,700
Trade receivables	48,325
Receivables allowance	(1,840)
	72,185

114 $45,100

	$
Trade payables	38,975
Bank overdraft	6,125
	45,100

115 C

	$
Accrual b/f	(327)
Amounts paid in the year	8,750
Expense (debit balance)	8,423

116 D

This entry will reduce receivables by the amount written off as irrecoverable.

117 C

	$	
Receivables b/f	83,200	
Less: irrecoverable w/off	(1,825)	
	81,375	
Allowance required	6,510	
Allowance b/f	8,200	
Reduction in allowance	1,690	i.e. a credit

118 B

119 $7,100

	$
Opening capital	18,000
Capital introduced	6,000
Drawings	(10,000)
Loss for the year – bal fig	**(7,100)**
Closing capital	6,900

120 $672.00

121 $5,675

	$
Opening liability	(4,275)
Paid in year	4,100
Output tax $90,000 @20%	(18,000)
Input tax $75,000 @ 20/120	12,500
Closing liability	(5,675)

122 B

	$
Payables	3,115
Bank overdraft	350
	3,465

123 $8,200

	$
Motor vehicles	7,200
Fixtures and fittings	1,000
	8,200

124 $3,260

	$	$
Sales		21,370
Cost of sales		(12,413)
Gross profit		8,957
Less: expenses		
Salaries and wages	3,560	
Motor expenses	572	
Rent and rates (600 + 150)	750	
Lighting and heating	702	
Sundry expenses	113	(5,697)
Profit for the year		3,260

125 D

	$
Inventory	5,243
Receivables	6,715
Cash at bank	115
	12,073

126 D

127 $583,000

	$	$
Balance b/f	84,700	
Credit sales – bal fig	583,000	
Cash received re credit sales		564,250
Contra with payables		8,300
Irrecoverable receivables		12,650
Balance c/f		82,500
Profit for the year	667,700	667,700

Note that the allowance for receivables is not relevant when preparing a receivables general ledger account. It is accounted for in a separate general ledger account.

128 C

129 $18,000

	$	$
Sales		180,000
Cost of sales:		
Opening inventory	20,000	
Purchases	160,000	
Less: closing inventory – bal fig	(18,000)	(162,000)
Gross profit 10% of sales		18,000

130 $23,832

	$
Opening capital	89,627
Profit for the year	32,678
Less: drawings – bal fig	(23,832)
Closing capital	98,473

131 B

If an item has been wrongly accounted for as an expense, it means that profit for the year will be reduced i.e. understated. It also means that the amount should be added to the value of assets on the statement of financial position. Until the adjustment is made, assets will also be understated.

132 $38,921

	$
Non-current assets	33,750
Inventory	4,845
Trade receivables	11,248
Trade payables	(9,633)
Bank overdraft	(539)
	39,671
Less: accrual	(750)
	38,921

133 C

134 $10,250

	$
Balance 1 January 20X5	10,250
Profit for the year	8,500
Capital introduced	3,800
Drawings	(7,300)
Balance 31 December 20X5	15,250

135 $55,842

	$
Trade receivables	55,742
Petty cash	100
	55,842

136 C

Trade discount is always deducted when calculating the amount invoiced by the seller. In addition, as Smith is not expected to take account of the early settlement discount terms, the amount of revenue receivable is calculated after deduction of trade discount only $950. ($1,000 × 95%). When Smith subsequently pays early to be eligible for the discount, the accounting entries should reflect that fact and record settlement of the amount outstanding and also a reduction in revenue.

Debit Cash $912 ($950 × 96%), Debit Revenue $38 ($950 × 4%), and Credit Trade receivables $950.

137 B

Trade discount is always deducted when calculating the amount invoiced by the seller. In addition, as Jones is expected to take account of the early settlement discount terms, the amount of revenue receivable is calculated after deduction of both trade discount and early settlement discount, a total of $2,280 ($2,500 × 95% × 96%). When Jones subsequently pays early to be eligible for the discount, the accounting entries should reflect the receipt of cash and clearance of the trade receivable for the amount expected.

Debit Cash $2,280 and Credit Trade receivables $2,280.

138 D

Trade discount is always deducted when calculating the amount invoiced by the seller. In addition, as Black is expected to take account of the early settlement discount terms, the amount of revenue receivable is calculated after deduction of both trade discount and early settlement discount, a total of $4,104 ($4,500 × 95% × 96%). When Black subsequently pays outside of the settlement discount period, the full amount of the receivable after trade discount of $4,275 ($4,500 × 95%) is due. The additional cash received in excess of the receivable amount of $171 is therefore accounted for as receipt of additional revenue.

Debit Cash $4,275, Credit Revenue $171, and Credit Trade receivables $4,104.

139 A

Trade discount is always deducted when calculating the amount invoiced by the seller. In addition, as White is not expected to take account of the early settlement discount terms, the amount of revenue receivable is calculated after deduction of trade discount only, a total of \$3,515 (\$3,700 × 95%). When White subsequently pays outside of the settlement discount period as expected, the full amount of the receivable is due.

140 A

Trade discount is always deducted when calculating the amount invoiced by the seller. In addition, as Green is expected to take account of the early settlement discount terms, the amount of revenue receivable is calculated after deduction of trade discount and early settlement discount, a total of \$1,276.80 (\$1,400 × 96% × 95%). When Green subsequently pays outside of the settlement discount period, the full amount of \$1,344 (\$1,400 × 96%) is due and the additional amount received of \$67.20 (\$1,344.00 – \$1,276.80) is accounted for as receipt of additional revenue.

Debit Cash \$1,344.00, Credit Revenue \$67.20, and Credit Trade receivables \$1,276.80.

INVENTORIES

141 B

142 \$40,755

	\$	\$
Cost of inventory		41,875
Damaged items:		
Cost	1,960	
Expected sale value	1,200	
Less cost of repairs	360	
Net realisable value	840	
Write down (\$1,960 – \$840)		1,120
Inventory valuation		40,755

143 \$3,567

Closing inventory is 160 units. Using FIFO, 150 of these are all deemed to be part of the final delivery, and therefore they are valued at \$22.30 per unit = \$3,345. The remaining 10 units are deemed to be part of the previous delivery and are therefore valued at \$22.20 per unit = \$222.

Thus total value is \$3,567

144 $3,648

	Units	Unit cost	Total cost
		$	$
Opening inventory	60	22.00	1,320.00
14 Aug Purchase	120	22.50	2,700.00
26 Aug Purchase	150	23.36	3,504.00
	330		7,524.00

Periodic weighted average cost per unit = $7,524.00/330 units = $22.80. Inventory valuation = 330 units – 170 sold = 160 × $22.80 = $3,648.00.

145 C

	Units	Unit cost	Total cost
		$	$
Opening inventory	60	22.00	1,320.00
14 Feb Purchase	180	23.00	4,140.00
	240	22.75	5,460.00
18 Feb Sale	(90)	22.75	(2,047.50)
Closing inventory	150	22.75	3,412.50

Note that, using the continuous weighted average method of inventory valuation, a new weighted average cost per unit is calculated following each purchase made.

146 $6,825

	Units	Unit cost	Total cost
		$	$
Opening inventory	120	22.00	2,640.00
15 Apr Purchase	360	23.00	8,280.00
	480	22.75	10,920.00
25 Apr Sale at cost	(300)	22.75	(6,825.00)
Closing inventory	180	22.75	4,095.00

Note that, using the continuous weighted average method of inventory valuation, a new weighted average cost per unit is calculated following each purchase made. The updated weighted average cost per unit is then used for each sale until the next purchase is made and the process is repeated.

147 $500

Inventory should be valued at the lower of cost and net realisable value. Net realisable values $1,200 – $250 = $950, with cost of $500 the lower of the two possibilities.

148 C

	$
Value at 7 July 20X6	38,950
Sales since year end (100/125 × $6,500)	5,200
Purchase since year end	(4,250)
Value at 30 June 20X6	39,900

149 A

The net realisable value of inventory items is the selling price less the 4% commission payable.

	NRV	Lower of cost or NRV
	$	$
Henry VII	2,784	2,280
Dissuasion	3,840	3,840
John Bunion	1,248	1,248
		7,368

150 D

The closing inventory of 12 items (15 – 5 + 10 – 8) comprise

	$
10 items at $3.50 each	35.00
2 items at $3 each	6.00
Cost on a FIFO basis is	41.00

151 B

The damaged items have a cost of $3,660, but a net realisable value of only $1,050 ($1,500 – $450). Therefore the cost of the inventory needs to be written down by $2,610 ($3,660 – $1,050). The inventory will then have a correct value of $36,140 ($38,750 – $2,610).

152 B

153 D

Closing inventory reduces the cost of sales figure. If the value of closing inventory is increased, cost of sales will be reduced and net profit will be increased. Net assets will also increase.

154 B

The over-valuation in 20X4 will boost profits in 20X4 by reducing cost of sales. However, the opening inventories in the following year will be overstated increasing cost of sales and reducing profits.

155 $15,800

Inventories are valued at the lower of cost and net realisable value. The cost of repairing the clock will reduce the expected profit, but the clock's net realisable value is still greater then cost and so no reduction in value is needed.

156 $9.4M

$6.5m + $1.6m + $1.3m = $9.4m

157 C

Administrative costs are not included in the statement of financial position valuation of an item in the inventory.

158 B

159 $12.50

Assuming that all the costs would be incurred by the seller (and not the customer) the net realisable value is $20 – $2 – $3 – $2.50 = $12.50.

160 $87,700

	$
Payments for purchases	85,400
Less: Invoices for opening inventory	(1,700)
Plus: Invoices due for fuel purchased	1,300
Purchases	85,000

	$
Opening inventory	12,500
Purchases	85,000
Closing inventory	(9,800)
Cost of fuel used in the year – profit or loss	87,700

161 $4,700

	Net realisable value	Lower of cost or NRV	Units	Value
	$	$		$
Basic	8	6	200	1,200
Super	8	8	250	2,000
Luxury	10	10	150	1,500
Total value				4,700

162 B

With FIFO, closing inventory is the most recently purchased items, therefore when prices are rising, closing inventory will have a higher value than if the average cost method of inventory valuation is used. Since closing inventories will be valued higher, the cost of sales will be lower and the profit will be higher.

163 $21,510

22,960 – 1,950 – 400 + 900 = $21,510

164 $22,030

22,700 – 1,300 + 700 – 70 = $22,030

165 C

166 $3,420

Continuous average cost per unit = ($815+= (270 × $19.50))/320 units = $19.00. Therefore cost of goods sold = 180 × 180 units = $3,420.

167 D

This double-entry reflects that fact that some of the purchases made for resale have now been taken by the proprietor for own use, and therefore an increase in drawings is also recorded.

168 B

The error has resulted in closing inventory (a debit balance in the statement of financial position) being overstated, with a corresponding overstatement in the credit entry made in the statement of profit or loss. Therefore, to correct this error, it requires a credit entry to Closing inventory (Statement of FP) to reduce the value of the inventory asset in the statement of financial position and a debit entry in the inventory account in the statement of P&L. The latter accounting entry has the effect of reducing the credit relating to closing inventory in the statement of P&L.

169 C

NON-CURRENT ASSETS AND DEPRECIATION

170 D

If a business is a going concern, it is reasonable to assume that non-current assets will be used over their expected useful economic life. It is therefore appropriate to value a non-current asset at cost less accumulated depreciation, which represents the consumption of value so far.

171 C

Depreciation spreads the value of a non-current asset over its expected useful life.

172 B

Year 1 charge = \$100,000 × 20% = \$20,000, leaving a book value of \$80,000.

Year 2 charge = \$80,000 × 20% = \$16,000.

173

	Selected answer
To calculate the total balance outstanding on loans raised to purchase non-current assets	
To help in carrying out the physical verification of non-current assets	Correct
To calculate the profit or loss on disposal of non-current assets	Correct
To eliminate the need to maintain ledger accounts relating to non-current assets	

174

	Selected answer
Cost of staff training to use the new plant and equipment	
Installation costs	Correct
Three-year maintenance agreement	
Delivery costs	Correct

Delivery and installation costs are incurred in getting the asset into working condition, and so they are capitalised. The maintenance costs merely maintain the asset, they do not improve it. Staff training costs can never be capitalised. Therefore they are charged as an expense.

175 $87,500

	$
Carrying amount of assets at start of year (140,000 – 60,000)	80,000
Assets purchased in the year	30,000
	110,000

	$
Depreciation at 25% of this balance: charge for the year	27,500
Opening balance, accumulated depreciation	60,000
Therefore closing balance	87,500

176 D

A non-current asset register is a detailed schedule of non-current, and is not another name for non-current asset ledger accounts in the general ledger.

177 A

The general ledger account for non-current assets shows a carrying amount that is $10,000 higher than the figure in the non-current assets register. This could be due to having omitted to deduct an asset with a carrying amount of $10,000 from the ledger. A non-current asset will have a carrying amount on disposal when it is sold for $15,000 and the profit on disposal is $5,000.

178 D

		$	
Proceeds		4,430	
Less carrying amount	(12,000 – 5,856)	(6,144)	
		1,714	loss

179 $3,200

The total cost of the asset is $16,000 ($11,570 cash plus the $4,430 trade-in allowance). $16,000 × 20% = $3,200.

180

	15% straight-line	**15% reducing balance**
Asset 1		Correct
Asset 2	Correct	

Asset 1 – ($100,000 – $50,000) × 15% = $7,500 calculated using the reducing balance basis.

Asset 2 – ($50,000 × 15%) = $7,500 calculated using the straight-line basis.

181 A

182 $1,984

Year ended	**Depreciation**	**Carrying amount c/f**
31 October 20X4	\$15,500 × 20% = \$3,100	\$15,500 – \$3,100 = \$12,400
31 October 20X5	\$12,400 × 20% = \$2,480	\$12,400 – \$2,480 = \$9,920
31 October 20X6	\$9,920 × 20% 1= \$1,984	

183 D

184 D

Cost \$80,000 and depreciation at 15% pa straight line is \$12,000

A full year's depreciation will be charged in the years to 30 September 20X5, 20X6 and 20X7. Therefore, the carrying amount is \$44,000. If proceeds are \$39,000, there will be a loss of \$5,000

185 $50,600

	\$
Cost of plant	48,000
Delivery	400
Modifications	2,200
	50,600

186 B

		\$
Year 1	Cost	2,400.0
	Depreciation at 20%	(480.0)
Year 2	Carrying value	1,920.0
	Depreciation at 20%	(384.0)
Year 3	Carrying value	1,536.0
	Depreciation at 20%	(307.2)
Year 4	Carrying value	1,228.8
	Sale proceeds	1,200.0
	Loss on disposal	(28.8)

187 $118,000

	$	$
Original balance		125,000
Carrying amount of asset sold:		
Proceeds	9,000	
Less: Profit	(2,000)	
		(7,000)
Adjusted balance		118,000

188 $360

	$
Cost	5,000
Year 1 (20% × 5,000)	(1,000)
Year 2 (20% × 4,000)	(800)
Year 3 (20% × 3,200)	(640)
Carrying amount at time of disposal	2,560
Sale proceeds	2,200
Loss on disposal	360

189 D

	Selected answer
The purchase of a car for a member of the sales department to visit clients	Correct
The purchase of a car for resale by a car dealer	
Legal fees incurred on the purchase of a building	Correct
The cost of painting a building	

The purchase of a car for resale means that the car is an item of inventory for the business, not a non-current asset. Legal fees incurred in purchasing a building are included in the cost of the building, and so is part of the non-current asset cost, i.e. asset expenditure. The cost of maintenance (i.e. painting a building) is an expense. The cost of purchasing a car for use by an employee performing their work duties should be capitalised.

190 $200

NCA Disposal

	$		$
Cost	12,000	Accumulated depreciation	7,200
		(3 yrs × 20% × $12,000)	
Profit (β)	200	Proceeds (part-exchange allowance)	5,000
	12,200		12,200

191 B

If an amount has been wrongly capitalised, rather than treated as an expense, the profit for the year will be higher than it should be. In addition, assets are overstated as they include an amount that should not have been capitalised.

192 C

If an amount has been wrongly accounted for as an expense, rather than capitalised, the profit for the year will be lower than it should be. In addition, assets are understated as they exclude an amount that should have been capitalised and accounted for as a non-current asset.

193 $6,000

NCA Disposal

	$		$
Cost	100,000	20X2 dep'n (100,000 × 20%)	20,000
Profit (β)	6,000	20X3 dep'n (800,000 × 20%)	16,000
		Disposal proceeds	70,000
	106,000		106,000

194 $6,250

NCA Disposal

	$		$
Cost	100,000	20X2 dep'n (90,000 × 15%)	15,000
		20X3 dep'n (90,000 × 15%)	15,000
		20X4 dep'n (90,000 × 15% × 3/12)	3,750
		Disposal proceeds	60,000
		Loss on disposal (β)	6,250
	100,000		100,000

195 $90,800

Depreciation

		$			$
	Disposal	17,200	1/1/X7	Bal b/d	92,000
31/12/X7	Bal c/d	90,800	31/12/X7	Profit or loss statement	16,000
		108,000			108,000
			1/1/X8	Bal b/d	90,800

196 $2,000

Disposal

		$			$
	Cost	20,000		Dep'n	17,200
31/12/X7	Profit or loss	2,000		Bank	4,800
		22,000			22,000

197 $16,000

Cost

		$			$
1/1/X7	Bal b/d	180,000		Disposal	20,000
			31/12/X7	Bal c/d	160,000
		180,000			180,000

NCA Cost $160,000 × 10% = $16,000 = depreciation charge

198 D

Disposal

		$			$
	Cost	20,000		Dep'n	17,200
31/12/X7	Profit or loss	2,000		Bank	4,800
		22,000			22,000

199 C

The gain or loss on disposal is the difference between the disposal value of the asset and its net book value at the date of disposal. If the asset's life and disposal value had been forecast with 100% accuracy, there would be no gain or loss on disposal.

200 $510,000

	Cost	Accum dep'n	CA
	$000	$000	$000
Opening balance	860	397	
Disposal	(80)	(43)	
	780	354	
Purchase	180		
Depreciation (10%)	960	96	
		450	
Carrying amount = 960 – 450			510

201 B

	$
Cost of asset	126,000
Depreciation to 31 October 20X3 (4/12 × 15%)	(6,300)
	119,700
Depreciation to 31 October 20X4 (15% × $119,700)	(17,955)
Depreciation to 31 October 20X5 (15% × $101,745)	(15,262)
Depreciation to 31 October 20X6 (15% × $86,483)	(12,972)
Depreciation to 30 September 20X7 (11/12 × 15% × $73,511)	(10,108)
Carrying amount at time of disposal	63,403
Disposal price	54,800
Loss on disposal	8,603

202 $1,836

Do not include the road tax in the cost of the car. Road tax is an expense item.

	$
Cost of asset	10,000
Depreciation 20X1 (25% × $10,000)	(2,500)
Depreciation 20X2 (25% × $7,500)	(1,875)
Depreciation 20X3 (25% × $5,625)	(1,406)
Depreciation 20X4 (25% × $4,219)	(1,055)
Carrying amount at date of disposal	3,164
Disposal value	5,000
Profit on disposal	1,836

203 $150,000

The asset disposed of had a net book value at the time of disposal = sales proceeds + loss on sale = $25,000 + $5,000 = $30,000.

	$
Carrying amount at 1 August 20X2	200,000
Carrying amount of asset disposed of	30,000
	170,000
Depreciation charge	20,000
Carrying amount at 31 July 20X3	150,000

204 A

You need to know the sales proceeds to calculate the length of ownership, or you need to know the length of ownership to calculate the sales proceeds. For example, this asset may have been sold after one year (NBV = $10,000) for $5,500, or it may have been sold after two years (NBV $8,000) for $3,500, and so on.

205 $87

	$
Cost of asset	9,000
Depreciation Year 1 (30% × $9,000)	(2,700)
Depreciation Year 2 (30% × $6,300)	(1,890)
Depreciation Year 3 (30%× $4,410)	(1,323)
Carrying amount at date of disposal	3,087
Disposal value	3,000
Loss on disposal	87

206 $100

	$
Sale value	5,300
Carrying amount (10,000 – 4,800)	5,200
	100

207 D

	$
Carrying amount (Cost – Accum dep'n) ($14,900 – $8,940)	5,960
Proceeds	7,455
= Profit	1,495

208 B

209 A

210 A

	Profit on disposal	**Loss on disposal**
Asset 1	Correct	
Asset 2		Correct

Asset 1: $7,500 – ($15,000 – $8,500) = $1,000 profit.

Asset 2: $6,500 – ($17,000 – $9,500) = $1,000 loss.

ACCRUALS AND PREPAYMENTS

211 $858,600

Rental income

	$		$
Balance b/f	42,300	Balance b/f	102,600
Statement of profit or loss (β)	**858,600**	Bank	838,600
Balance c/f	88,700	Balance c/f	48,400
	989,600		989,600

212 A

		$
Statement of profit or loss	9/12 × $10,800	8,100
	3/12 × $12,000	3,000
		11,100
Statement of financial position prepayment	9/12 × $12,000	9,000

213 D

Statement of profit or loss (5/12 × $24,000) + (7/12 × $30,000) = $27,500

Statement of financial position $7,500 paid on 1 January therefore amount prepaid by tenant is:

2/3 × $7,500 = $5,000. For Vine this is prepaid/deferred income, i.e. income received in advance – a liability.

214 $385

Motor expenses

		$		$
Balance b/f (insurance)		80	Balance b/f (petrol)	95
Cash paid	– petrol	95		
	– other bills	245	**Statement of profit or loss (β)**	**385**
Balance c/f (petrol)		120	Balance c/f (insurance)	60
		540		540

The insurance prepayment covers 4 months as at the start of September. Therefore there must be a prepayment of 3 months at the end of September.

215 A

Charge to statement of profit or loss $1,800 × 7/12 = $1,050

Prepayment $1,800 × 5/12 = $750

216 C

The accrual for May and June 20X3 is assumed to be 2/3 × $840 = $560.

Electricity expenses

	$		$
Bank	600	Opening balance b/f	300
Bank	720		
Bank	900		
Bank	840		
Closing balance c/f	560	Statement of profit or loss	3,320
	3,620		3,620

217 B

The charge in the statement of profit or loss will be the amount of interest incurred from 1 January (when the loan was taken out) to 30 September (the year-end) i.e. 9/12 × 12% × $100,000 = $9,000. This represents three interest payments.

However, as only two interest payments were made (1 April and 1 July) the third payment due to be made on 1 October, which relates to the three months to 30 September, will be accrued: 3/12 × 12% × $100,000 = $3,000.

218 C

		$
Prepayment brought forward at the start of the year		10,000
Payment during the year		36,000
		46,000
Less:	Prepayment carried forward at the year end (7 months, therefore $36,000 × 7/12)	(21,000)
Charge for insurance in the statement of profit or loss		25,000

219 A

Accrued income is income not yet received for a service already provided (income received in arrears). Accounting for accrued income will therefore increase, rather than decrease, profit. A prepayment is an asset and an accrual is a liability.

220 B

The charge in the statement of profit or loss will be the amount of interest incurred from 1 January (when the loan was taken out) to 31 March (the year-end) i.e. 3/12 × 10% × $250,000 = $6,250. This represents three months of accrued interest charges due to be paid on 1 April 20X3. This will also be the accrual in the statement of financial position as no payment has been made in the period to 31 March 20X3.

221 A

Tutorial note

- *The reduction in cash is replaced by an increase in prepayments and therefore assets remain unchanged.*
- *Liabilities are not affected and so remain unchanged.*
- *As Capital = Assets – Liabilities and both assets and liabilities remain unchanged, it remains that capital is unchanged.*

222 C

Rent of $7,800 paid in advance, thus prepayment at year end. At 30 November, two months of the period for which rent has been paid is unexpired.

Rent for one month = $7,800 ÷ 4 = $1,950

Two months paid in advance = $1,950 × 2 = $3,900

223 $1,813

Electricity account

	$		$
Paid in year	1,765	Opening balance	264
Closing balance	312	Charge for year	1,813 (bal fig)
	2,077		2,077

224 $1,268

The opening balance will represent the accrual of $1,268.

As this is an accrual (or liability), the opening trial balance will record a credit balance.

225 C

The total paid during the year is indicated by the bank transactions (3,000 + 3,000 + 3,600 + 3,600 = 13,200). The charge to profit or loss is shown as $13,000.

226 C

	$
5 months at ($24,000/12) per month	10,000
7 months at ($30,000/12) per month	17,500
Annual rent expense	27,500

227 A

Charge to the profit or loss: 7 months: 7/12 × $1,800 = $1,050

Prepayment of rent: 5 months: 5/12 × $1,800 = $750

228 C

Profit or loss charge for insurance: (7 months): 7/12 × $2,400 = $1,400

Prepayment: 5 months = 5/12 × $2,400 = $1,000

229 $3,300

The situation in the question is unusual because there is an opening accrual on the account, but a closing prepayment of 1/3 × $1,200 = $400.

Rent account

	$		$
Bank	4,000	Balance b/d (accrual)	300
		Profit or loss statement	3,300
		Balance c/d (prepayment)	400
	4,000		4,000

230 C

The accrual for May and June 20X3 is assumed to be 2/3 × $840 = $560.

Electricity expenses account

	$		$
Bank	600	Opening balance b/d	300
Bank	720		
Bank	900		
Bank	840		
Closing balance c/d	560	Statement of Profit or loss	3,320
	3,620		3,620
		Opening balance b/d	560

231 $12,600

Insurance for the year 1 July 20X2 to 30 June 20X3 was $13,200 × 1/1.1 = $12,000.

Profit or loss charge:

Six months at $12,000 plus six months at $13,200 = $6,000 + $6,600.= $12,600

232 $1,840

The rent payment covers the period 1 March to 31 August. At 30 June, there is a prepayment of two months (July and August). The amount of the prepayment is 2/6 × $5,520 = $1,840.

233 $1,400

There is an accrual for two months (October and November) during which electricity charges have been incurred but no invoice has been received yet. The best estimate of the accrual is 2/3 × $2,100 = $1,400.

234 B

A prepaid expense will reduce the charge to profit or loss. It will also be shown as a current asset in the statement of financial position.

235 C

The accrual should have been for $700, but was actually $1,400. Therefore it needs to be reduced by $700.

236 B

	$
Loss reported in draft accounts	(1,486)
Less accrual (an additional expense)	(1,625)
Add back prepayment (a reduction in expenses)	834
Revised loss	(2,277)

237 D

Under the accruals concept, the accounts should include the cost of electricity consumed up to the end of the financial year. The charge for the last two months should be estimated, and included in the charge against profit. The best available estimate is based on the last bill, which indicates a monthly charge of $1,090. Thus the total accrual is $2,180.

238 B

The opening trial balance will reflect the liability brought forward. (The charge to profit or loss has been written off, and is therefore eliminated from the expense account.)

239

	Accrual	**Prepayment**
Repairs and renewals		Correct
Light and heat	Correct	

Repairs and renewals: $39,500 – $2,000 – $36,500 = $1,000 prepayment.

Light and heat: $25,000 – $1,000 – $25,500 = $1,500 accrual.

RECEIVABLES, PAYABLES AND PROVISIONS

240 $5,350

		Allowance	Expense
	$	$	$
Receivables balance (draft)	58,200		
Irrecoverable debts	(8,900)		8,900
	49,300		
Specific allowance:	(1,350)	1,350	
	(750)	750	
	47,200		
Allowance c/f		2,100	
Allowance b/f		5,650	
Decrease in allowance		3,550	(3,550)
Total expense			5,350

241 $13,450

Receivables

	$		$
Balance b/f (W)	13,150		
Sales	125,000	Bank	115,500
		Irrecoverable debts	7,100
		Balance c/f	15,550
	138,150		138,150

	b/f	c/f
	$	$
Gross receivables	13,150	15,550
Allowance	(1,150)	(2,100)
Net receivables	12,000	13,450

242 B

The write off of debts will reduce the gross receivables balance by $72,000 to $766,000. The allowance is to be adjusted to $60,000 (hence an adjustment of $12,000).

The net balance is therefore $766,000 less $60,000, i.e. $706,000.

243 $5,083

Year-end receivables	5% × $7,000,000	=	$350,000
Year-end allowance for receivables		=	$14,000
Allowance at start of year		=	$11,667
Increase in allowance		=	**$2,333**

Note that the irrecoverable debts had been written off during the year and have already been excluded from the receivables balance at 30 September 20X8.

Irrecoverable debts expense

	$		$
Write off of irrecoverable debts	3,200	Recovery of irrecoverable debts	450
Increase in allowance	2,333	Statement of profit or loss (β)	5,083
	5,533		5,533

244 B

245 C

246 D

247 D

248 B

249 B

250 A

251 C

252 $20,200

Trade receivables

	$		$
Balance b/f	10,000	Bank	90,000
Sales	100,000	Irrecoverable in year	800
Irrecoverable debts recovered	1,000	Balance c/f	20,200
	111,000		111,000

253 A

When a debt is written off as irrecoverable, the transaction is recorded as:

Dr Irrecoverable debts account (expense), and Cr Receivables

Any subsequent change to the allowance for receivables should be dealt with as a separate matter.

254 $340,750

Cash sales do not affect receivables. Discounts received affect payables, not receivables. The allowance for receivables does not affect the amount of receivables, but specific irrecoverable debts written off do affect receivables.

Receivables

	$		$
Balance b/f	37,500	Contra with payables	1,750
Sales (credit)	357,500	Irrecoverable debts written off	3,500
		Bank (β)	340,750
		Balance c/f	49,000
	395,000		395,000

255 $800

	$
Irrecoverable debts written off (800 + 550)	1,350
Irrecoverable debt recovered	(350)
Reduction in allowance for receivables	(200)
Charge to statement of profit or loss	800

256 B

The allowance for receivables will reduce the book value of receivables. An increase in an allowance for receivables will therefore reduce net current assets.

257 $5,270

	$	$
Receivables balance	230,000	
Specific allowance – Em	(450)	450
– Lu	(980)	980
– Sandy	(5,000)	5,000
	228,570	
Total allowance at end of year c/f		6,430
Allowance b/f		(11,700)
Decrease in allowance = Cr to statement of profit or loss		5,270

288 A

The net amount reported in the statement of financial position is $47,744 due less the $3,500 allowance for doubtful debts.

259 $2,000

The charge for irrecoverable debts and allowance for receivables is the actual amount of bad debts written off plus the increase in the allowance for doubtful debts, or minus the decrease in the allowance.

	$
Allowance required at end of year	6,000
Allowance required at start of year	9,000
Decrease in allowance	(3,000)
Irrecoverable debts written off	5,000
Charge to profit or loss	2,000

260 $158

	$
Allowance required	5,512
Less: opening allowance	(5,670)
Decrease (credit) recognised in profit or loss	(158)

261 B

262 D

263 C

264 B

265 $1,500

If, on average, five microwave ovens are returned in the month following sale, and refunds are made in that month, only expected returns in January 20X6 from sales made in December 200X5 will require a provision. This will be $1,500 ($300 × 5).

266 C

The statement of profit or loss will include the movement in the provision from one reporting date to the next. In this case, the provision needs to be reduced by $1,608 ($6,548 – $4,940) which will result in a credit to the statement of profit or loss.

267 A

The statement of profit or loss will include the movement in the provision from one reporting date to the next. In this case, the provision needs to be increased by $800 which will result in a charge to the statement of profit or loss and an increase in the provision in the statement of financial position.

268 C

Provision required	$7,634	
Provision brought forward	$6,548	
Increase in provision	$1,086	increase in provision = charge

269 B

The provision has decreased by $500.

CAPITAL AND FINANCE COSTS

270 D

271 $7,000

	$
Capital balance b/f	12,000
Capital introduced in the year	1,500
Profit (loss) for the year **bal fig**	7,000
Drawings	(6,000)
Capital balance c/f	14,500

272 $23,000

	$
Capital balance b/f	12,000
Capital introduced in the year **bal fig**	23,000
Profit (loss) for the year	(13,000)
Drawings	(7,500)
Capital balance c/f	14,500

273 $15,300

	$
Capital balance b/f	23,000
Capital introduced in the year	3,000
Profit (loss) for the year	(2,500)
Drawings	(8,200)
Capital balance c/f **bal fig**	15,300

274 $9,600

	$
Capital balance b/f	35,000
Profit (loss) for the year **bal fig**	9,600
Drawings	(14,600)
Capital balance c/f	30,000

275 $41,650

	$
Capital balance b/f **bal fig**	41,650
Capital introduced in the year	2,750
Profit (loss) for the year	13,800
Drawings	(15,700)
Capital balance c/f	42,500

276 $7,700

	$
Capital balance b/f	12,735
Profit (loss) for the year **bal fig**	(7,700)
Drawings	(2,345)
Balance c/f	2,690

277 C

Liabilities should also include six months of interest accrued of $300 ($7,500 × 8% × 6/12).

278 $15,000

	$
Capital balance b/f	28,350
Capital introduced in the year	3,000
Profit (loss) for the year	9,335
Drawings **bal fig**	(15,000)
Capital balance c/f	25,685

279 $14,750

	$
Capital balance b/f	18,500
Capital introduced in the year **bal fig**	14,750
Profit (loss) for the year	(8,000)
Drawings	(8,500)
Capital balance c/f	16,750

280 C

RECONCILIATIONS

281 B

282 A

The cancelled cheques should be entered in the bank general ledger account by debiting $642.

283 $700

	$
Overdraft in bank statement	(38,600)
Deposits not yet credited to the account	41,200
	2,600
Cheques paid but not yet presented to the bank	(3,300)
Overdraft per bank ledger account (credit balance)	(700)

284

	Selected answer
Bank charges	Correct
Cheque not presented	
A dishonoured cheque from a customer	Correct
Deposits not credited	

An entry is required in the bank ledger account for all correct items in the bank statement that have not yet been recorded in the bank ledger account. These are the items that the business learns about when the bank statement is received, and should then record those items in its own accounting records. Such items include bank charges (including overdraft interest) and details of dishonoured cheques. Cheques not yet presented and deposits not yet credited have already been recorded in the bank ledger account.

285 B

Only the incorrectly recorded cheque requires a correcting entry. The unpresented cheque is just a timing difference.

286 B

287 D

The corrected general ledger balance should be reported on the statement of financial position. In this case, no adjustments are needed to the general ledger balance, as the reconciling items arise due to transactions being recorded at different times by the client and the bank (sometimes referred to as 'timing differences').

288 C

The ledger balance of $422 credit should be adjusted by a debit entry of $153 for interest. Thus the corrected balance is $269 credit. The statement balance will therefore be an overdraft of $269 after the cheque of $822 has been processed.

Therefore, the balance per the bank statement must be $553 credit (i.e. cash in the bank account).

289 D

290 B

	$
Cash at bak general ledger balance (debit, therefore cash in the bank)	25,000
Items not yet in the bank statement:	
Payments to suppliers	3,500
Payments into the account (lodgements)	(3,800)
Bank statement balance	24,700

291 C

	$
Overdraft per bank statement	(38,600)
Deposits not yet credited to the account	41,200
	2,600
Cheques paid but not yet presented to the bank	(3,300)
Overdraft per bank ledger account	(700)

292 B

	$
Opening balance	(89.93)
Interest	(16.45)
Closing balance	(106.38)

293 C

	$		$
Bank ledger balance	148	Corrected bank ledger	113
Bank charges	(10)	Unpresented cheques	125
Standing order	(25)	Outstanding lodgements	(85)
Corrected bank ledger	113	Bank statement balance	153

294 A

	$
Balance per bank statement	(210)
Less: unpresented cheques	(83)
Add: uncredited lodgements	30
Corrected balance per bank ledger	(263)

295 C

A credit in the bank statement is a debit entry in the bank general ledger account.

296 B

297

	True	False
If the bank statement balance and bank general ledger account balance is not identical as at a specific date, it means that there must be one or more errors in the general ledger account.		Correct
If the bank statement balance and bank general ledger account balance is not identical as at a specific date, it means that there must be one or more errors in the bank statement.		Correct

In both situations, it may be that there are timing differences, such as uncleared lodgements or cheques not yet presented. They are not errors; they are reconciling items

298 B

Pen Co believes that it owes $150 more than the supplier has stated. With items A, C and D, the result would be that the supplier will state that more is owed, not less, than Pen Co believes to be the case. If the supplier has recorded discount allowed to Pen Co, which it has not yet recorded, this will reduce the amount owed by Pen Co.

299 B

BNO Co apparently owes ANO Co $150 more than the supplier statement identifies. With items, A, C and D the result would be that the supplier will state that you owe more, not less. Item B is the only possible answer, which could explain the situation.

300 D

The numbers of invoices would be checked off against the statement and duplicate numbers should be identified. Errors in calculations and discounts should be identified when checking the invoices against orders. Non-delivery of items would be identified through the use of other records. Any discrepancies and errors would be communicated to the supplier.

301 C

302 D

	Payables' ledger	Supplier statement
	$	$
Per question	230	3,980
Cheque 1		(270)
Goods returned 2		(180)
Contra 3		(3,200)
Revised balance	230	330

Difference $100 (330 – 230)

303 B

	Lee's records
	$
Per question	14,500
Unrecorded discount	(150)
Revised balance = supplier statement	14,350

Lee Co believes that the amount owed is $150 more than the supplier has stated. Items A, C and D would result in a different outcome.

304 B

	$		$
Balance per payable ledger	260	Balance per supplier's statement	1,350
Cash discount disallowed	80	Less: Goods returned	(270)
		Less: Cash in transit	(830)
Adjusted payable ledger	340	Revised balance	250

Unreconciled difference = ($340 – $250) = $90

305 C

306 D

307 C

	$
Alpha – statement balance	3,465
Automated payment not recorded by Alpha	(690)
Invoice not recorded by Rome Co	(280)
Payable ledger account balance	2,495

308 D

	$		$
Beta – statement balance	4,278	Payable ledger balance	3,204
Automated payment not recorded by Beta	(784)	Invoice not recorded by Milan Co	280
	3,494		3,494

309 A

	$
Payable ledger account balance for Delta	6,045
Payment and discount not recorded on Delta statement	414
Goods returned not on Delta statement	105
Balance per statement issued by Delta	6,564

310 C

	$		$
Zeta – statement balance	9,613	Payable ledger balance	7,672
Automated payment not recorded by Zeta	(1,506)	Invoice not recorded by Portofino Co	435
	8,107		8,107

311 D

	$
Balance per statement issued by Theta	4,278
Contra not yet recorded on statement	(784)
Invoice not yet recorded by Genoa Co	(543)
Balance per Genoa Co payable ledger account for Theta	2,951

312 A

	$
Payable ledger account balance for Kappa	4,368
Discount not granted by Kappa	22
Goods returned not on Kappa statement	532
Balance per statement issued by Kappa	4,922

313 D

	$		$
Rho – statement balance	7,278	Payable ledger balance	5,639
Contra not yet recorded by Rho	(2,471)	Credit note not yet recorded by Lecce Co	(832)
	4,807		4,807

314 B

	$		$
Sigma – statement balance	4,684	Payable ledger balance	3,034
Bank payment not yet recorded	(1,342)	Credit note not yet recorded by Parma Co	(276)
		Invoice not yet recorded by Parma Co	584
	3,342		3,342

315 C

	$		$
Omega – statement balance	1,783	Payable ledger balance	1,213
Contra not yet recorded	(421)	Credit note not yet recorded by Turin Co	(92)
		Invoice not yet recorded by Turin Co	241
	1,362		1,362

316 A

	$		$
Tau – statement balance	5,432	Payable ledger balance	4,575
Invoice included in error	(875)	Credit note not yet recorded	(18)
	4,557		4,557

317 A

	$		$
Omicron – statement balance	8,314	Payable ledger balance	7,224
Automated payment	(2,546)	Invoice included in error	(1,456)
	5,768		5,768

318 C

There is no error in the general ledger. The error lies in the coding and allocation of the purchase invoice to the wrong payable ledger account.

319 D

The general ledger account for payables needs to be increased by $22 to reflect the fact that discount received previously recorded was not confirmed by the supplier. The opposite entry in the general ledger is to reduce discount received by $22. Remember that the payable ledger accounts of individual suppliers do not form part of the double-entry recording process in the general ledger.

320 B

The closing balance on the payables general ledger account will be a liability of $37,765.

321 C

	$		$
Phi – statement balance	8,866	Payable ledger balance	6,727
Automated payment not on statement	(1,605)	Invoice not yet recorded by Trento Co	534
	7,261		7,261

THE TRIAL BALANCE AND CORRECTION OF ERRORS

322 D

323 C

All three items are limitations of a trial balance.

Figures in the trial balance are not necessarily the final figures to be reported in the financial statements; they are subject to year-end adjustments.

Errors of commission (where an entry has been posted to the wrong account) are not identified by the trial balance since an equal debit and credit entry are still posted.

Although a trial balance can identify if double entry has broken down, it does not indicate in which accounts wrong entries were made.

324

	True	False
The trial balance provides a check that no errors exist in the accounting records of a business.		✓
The trial balance is one of the financial statements prepared annually by an entity for its shareholders.		✓

When a trial balance agrees, this does not confirm that no errors have been made in the accounting records. Postings to the wrong general ledger account could have occurred, perhaps by a coding error when transactions were processed. The trial balance is not one of the financial statements prepared by an entity for its shareholders.

325 D

General ledger account balance will be calculated automatically by the accounting system, rather than being a manual task performed by a member of the accounting department, which may lead to errors.

326 B

General ledger accounts may still contain duplicated transactions, or there may be omitted transactions from the balances which comprise the trial balance.

327 A

328 D

329 B

330 B

331 D

332 B

The buildings at cost is a non-current asset – a debit balance.

333 C

The capital account is a credit balance.

334 A

335 B

The payables account and the motor expenses account are affected by the error. Because the original entries were overstated by $36 then both accounts will also be overstated by $36 – both motor expenses are payables need to be reduced by this amount.

336

	True	**False**
A separate suspense account should be opened for each error in the general ledger		Correct
A suspense account is sometimes opened to complete postings whilst more information is sought on a transaction	Correct	

There is no need to open a separate suspense account for each error identified. Therefore the first statement is incorrect. A suspense account is sometimes used to complete a posting while further information is being sought, so the second statement is correct.

337 C

The debit entry in the payables' account was correctly recorded. The credit entry must have been made in the suspense account. To clear the suspense account requires the following:

Debit Suspense, and Credit Discount received

338 C

339 D

340 C

Suspense account

	$		$
Disposal of NCA	9,000	Balance b/d	9,000
	9,000		9,000

The initial debit entry to the cash at bank account was correctly accounted for. The credit entry must have been posted to suspense account. It therefore needs a debit entry to clear suspense, with the credit entry going to the disposal of non-current assets account to determine the profit on disposal.

341 C

Suspense account

	$		$
Balance b/d	1,300	Irrecoverable debts expense	1,300
	1,300		1,300

The initial credit entry to the allowance for receivables account had been recorded correctly. Therefore, the debit entry must have been posted to suspense account. To clear this, a credit entry to suspense account is required, with a debit entry in the irrecoverable debts expense account.

342 $50,101

	$
Profit or loss statement credit balances (income)	281,917
Profit or loss statement debit balances (expenses)	231,816
Profit for the year	50,101

343 $12,081

The debit profit or loss column exceeds the credit column by $12,081. This means that expenses have exceeded income, so the business has made a loss.

344 A

Error 1 – The entry should have been Debit Bank, Credit Receivables with simultaneous update of the customer account in the receivables' ledger. The general ledger accounts were updated correctly, only the reference to the individual customer account was wrong. This should be corrected by journal adjustment which will not require a suspense account.

Error 2 – The omission of a transaction does not need a suspense account to correct it.

345 C

Neither error 1 nor error 2 require a suspense account to be corrected.

346 D

347 D

	Dr	**Cr**
	$	$
Sales		258,542
Opening inventory	9,649	
Purchases	142,958	
Expenses	34,835	
Non-current assets at carrying amount	63,960	
Receivables	31,746	
Payables		13,864
Cash at bank	1,783	
Capital		12,525
	$284,931	$284,931

348 B

For the statement of profit or loss, the total of the credit column exceeds the total of the debit column by $22,689. This represents the profit.

349 B

350 C

351 D

352 A

353 D

354 B

355 C

PREPARING FINANCIAL STATEMENTS

356 C

The depreciation expense is charged (debited) to profit or loss. The accumulated depreciation is a credit balance in the statement of financial position, reducing the carrying amount of the related non-current assets.

357 B

The allowance for receivables is a credit balance, which is offset against receivables within current assets in the statement of financial position and the irrecoverable debts account is an expense account (debit balance) in the statement of profit or loss.

358 B

This is an example of an irrecoverable debt being written off. This requires a credit to the receivables account in order to clear the debt and debit the bad debts account with the amount of the debt written off.

359 A

360 C

	$
Allowance required	890
Allowance brought forward	770
Increase	120

As the allowance has increased, a charge is made to profit or loss.

361 B

The receipt has been accounted for: Debit Bank, and Credit Receivables.

It should have been accounted for as: Debit Bank, and Credit Irrecoverable debts.

(The receivable was removed from the accounts when the irrecoverable debt was written off. The receipt is the recovery of an irrecoverable debt, which is credited to the irrecoverable debts account.)

To correct the error: Debit: Receivables, and Credit: Irrecoverable debts.

362 C

Syl still has to pay the phone bill for November and this must be reflected in the accounts.

(⅓ × $1,800) = $600 (accrued expenses)

363 A

The profit will be reduced by $250 to $24,702 by the inclusion of the invoice in expenses. As profit is reduced, the capital balance will also be reduced by $250 (to $75,591).

364 D

365 B

366 D

Invoice to 30 September $462 for three months, thus charge is $154 per month.

Accounts to 30 November, thus two months accrued = $308.

Charge = $1,540 + $308 = $1,848

367 C

The capital amount is paid at the end of the loan term – it is a non-current liability. Interest is incurred on a 'day-by-day' basis and, at the reporting date, no unpaid liability for interest has been incurred.

368 A

Allowance required	$2,757
Existing allowance	$2,492
Increase, therefore charge	$265

369 B

Receivables' balance ($137,850) less revised allowance ($2,757) = $135,093.

370 A

The cost of inventory includes carriage inwards (carriage outwards is classified as a selling and distribution expense). Irrecoverable debts written off and any movement in the allowance for receivables are not part of cost of sales: they are expenses.

371 D

If expenses are incorrectly classified as asset expenditure, both the net profit and the net assets will be overstated. Net profit is overstated as only depreciation is deducted rather than the full cost of the expense. Net assets are overstated because expenses have been incorrectly included.

372

	Current asset	**Non-current asset**
Assets which will be converted into cash as part of normal business activity	Correct	
Assets which are used to increase productive capacity of the business		Correct

Current assets, such as inventories or trade receivables, are normally converted into cash within 12 months.

373 B

Current		$
Payments due:	1 November 20X5	3,000
	1 May 20X6	3,000
		6,000
Long term:	balance	21,000
Total		27,000

374 C

375 A

The trade receivables balance net of any allowance is reported as a current asset.

376 C

377 A

378 C

379 D

380 $105,946

Tutorial note

It may be useful to consider this as a T account. Remember to include the irrecoverable debts and contra should be on the credit side of the receivables account as they are offset against sales made in the year. Do use workings to answer multiple choice questions where necessary.

Trade receivables

Balance b/f	30,468	Cash received	105,382
Sales (balancing figure)	105,946	Contra with payables	1,000
		Irrecoverable debts	2,500
		Balance c/f	27,532
	136,414		136,414

381 C

382 C

383 A

Trade receivables

Balance b/f	20,000	Cash received	5,000
Sales (balancing figure)	9,000	Irrecoverable debts	1,500
		Balance c/f	22,500
	29,000		29,000

384 $93,582

The opening balance is $2,304 more than the closing balance. Purchases are $2,304 less than the payments, i.e. $93,582.

Tutorial note

It may be easier to consider this as a T account. Do use workings to answer multiple choice questions where necessary.

Trade payables

		B/f	13,856
Cash paid	95,886	Purchases (balancing figure)	93,582
C/f	11,552		

385 $98,995

Sales represent 125% of the cost of sales

Thus cost of sales = $120,600 × 100/125 = $96,480

Inventory value increased by $2,515

Thus purchases were $96,480 + $2,515 = $98,995

386 $280

Contras are the balancing figure in the receivables general ledger account after all other items have been included in the account. Note that the allowance for receivables does not directly affect the receivables account.

Receivables

	$		$
Balance b/d	800	Bank	6,730
Sales	6,800	Irrecoverable debts	40
		Payables contras	280
		Balance c/d	550
	7,600		7,600
Balance b/d	550		

387 C

	$
Cash owed by customers at the year end	1,300
Cash from clients during the year	28,000
	29,300
Cash owed by customers at the start of the year	(800)
Therefore sales in the year	28,500

388 A

	$
Cash owed to suppliers at the year end	200
Payments to suppliers during the year	1,800
	2,000
Payables at the start of the year	(70)
Therefore purchases in the year	1,930

389 B

	Carrying amount		Depreciation
	$		$
Furniture		(25% of 800)	200
Computer	1,575	(× 25%)	394
Printer	844	(× 25%)	211
			805

390 A

	Cost	Accumulated dep'n	Carrying amount
	$	$	$
Furniture	800	400	400
Computer	2,800	1,619	1,181
Printer	1,500	867	633
	5,100	2,886	2,214
Inventories		900	
Receivables		1,300	
Bank (see note)		3,900	
		6,100	
Payables		(200)	5,900
			8,114
Bank loans (2,400 + 2,000)			(4,400)
Net assets = Capital			3,714

Receipts = 30,000. Payments = 26,800. Cash at start of year = $700. Therefore cash at year-end = 700 + 30,000 – 26,800 = 3,900.

391 B

	$
Capital at end of year	3,714
Capital at start of year	2,599
Increase in capital	1,115
Add back: Drawings	24,000
Profit for the year	25,115

392 $18,950

	$
Sales	230,000
Money banked (160,000 + 50,000)	210,000
	20,000
Increase in receivables (3,000 – 2,000)	(1,000)
Increase in cash in till (100 – 50)	(50)
Money unaccounted for = stolen	18,950

393 $183,279

	$	
Opening payables	28,754	
Add purchases during the year	183,279	**Balancing figure**
Less payments during the year	(185,844)	
Closing payables	26,189	

394 $14,790

		$
Opening inventory		15,740
Add purchases during the year		75,550
Less COST of goods sold during the year	$\frac{100}{120}$ × $91,800	(76,500)
Closing inventory		14,790

395 $700

Sales = $10,000 × 50% × 1.2 = $6,000

Cost of sales = $10,000 × 50% = ($5,000)

Commission = $6,000 × 5% = ($300)

Net profit = $700

396 $129,935

Purchases were	payments made plus increase in suppliers' balances			
	i.e. $127,569 + ($12,826 – $11,564)		=	$128,831
Thus cost of sales	Opening inventory	$5,288		
	Purchases	$128,831		
		$134,119		
	– Closing inventory	$4,184	=	$129,935

397 B

398 B

399 $104,902

> ***Tutorial note***
>
> *It may be useful to consider this as a T account. Remember to include the discounts received and the contra with the receivables account. Do use workings to answer multiple choice questions where necessary.*

Trade payables

		B/f	24,786
Cash paid	104,886	Purchases (balancing figure)	104,902
Contra with receivables	500		
Discount received	750		
C/f	23,552		
	129,688		129,688

400 A

401 A

Trade receivables

Balance b/f	29,100	Cash received	381,600
Refunds to customers	2,100	Expenses paid by cash	6,800
Sales (balancing figure)	412,400	Contras with payables	9,400
		Amounts written off	7,200
		Balance c/f	38,600
	443,600		443,600

Total sales = $412,400 + $11,900 = $525,300

402 D

	%	$
Sales revenue	120	240,600
Cost of sales	100	200,500
Gross profit	20	40,100

Need to adjust cost of sales for opening and closing inventory for the cost of purchases.

Purchases = $200,500 + $17,855 – $13,340 = $205,015.

403 A

Tutorial note

It may be useful to consider this as a T account. Remember to include the irrecoverable debt and the contras with the trade payables account.

Trade receivables

Balance b/f	22,785	Cash received	95,723
Sales (balancing figure)	101,718	Contras with payables	3,750
		Amount written off	350
		Balance c/f	24,680
	124,503		124,503

404 B

Tutorial note

It may be useful to consider this as a T account. Remember that if an amount has already been written-off as irrecoverable, it must be removed from the receivables account. Discounts received relate to early settlement of amounts due to trade payables and is not relevant in this situation.

Trade receivables

Balance b/f	32,785	Cash received	87,654
Sales (balancing figure)	87,312	Contra with payables	2,193
		Amount written off	127
		Balance c/f	30,123
	120,097		120,097

405 C

Tutorial note

Remember to separate the proceeds from the disposal of the asset as this is not a sales receipt – it will be used to calculate the profit or loss on disposal of that asset.

Cash account

Balance b/f	250	Banking	34,200
Cash sales (balancing figure)	36,050	Wages	3,500
Asset disposal proceeds	3,250	Drawings	1,500
		Balance c/f	350
	39,550		39,550

406 D

Cash account

Balance b/f	70	Banking	87,654
Cash sales (balancing figure)	88,959	Wages	8,750
Capital introduced	10,000	Drawings	1,825
		Laptop purchased	750
		Balance c/f	50
	99,029		99,029

407 A

Cash account

Balance b/f	100	Banking	67,890
Cash sales (balancing figure)	79,418	Wages	6,750
		Drawings	500
		Repair	350
		Purchases	3,728
		Returned goods refund	100
		Balance c/f	200
	79,518		79,518

To arrive at the sales figure for the month, remember to deduct the refund from the total of sales receipts: $79,418 – $100 = $79,318.

408 $33,773

Cash account

Balance b/f	70	Banking	26,543
Cash sales (balancing figure)	33,773	Wages	3,750
		Drawings	1,750
		Furniture	1,750
		Balance c/f	50
	33,843		33,843

409 $661,900

Cost of sales = $825,000 × 100/125 = $660,000. To word back to the purchases cost, adjust cost of sales for opening and closing inventory value = $660,000 – $12,800 + $14,700 = $661,900.

410 $125,103

Trade payables

Payments made	123,456	Balance b/f	21,876
Discount received	1,025	Purchases (balancing figure)	125,103
Contra with receivables	2,500		
Balance c/f	19,998		
	146,979		146,979

411 B

	$
Required allowance for receivables	3,600
Allowance last year ($3,600 × 100/125)	2,880
Increase in allowance	720
Irrecoverable debts written off	3,200
Irrecoverable debts recovered	(150)
Charge to profit or loss	3,770

412 C

	$
Allowance for receivables at start of year:	630
Required allowance at end of year	525
Reduction in allowance (credit profit or loss)	105

413 B

	$
Irrecoverable debts written off	18,000
Reduction in allowance for receivables	(17,000)
Net charge for irrecoverable debts and allowance for receivables	1,000

A charge is an expense, which is a debit item.

414 B

Receivables balances	$37,890	
Less: write off	$1,570	
Revised receivables	$36,320	
Less: allowance req'd	$1,158	(i.e. allowance required at 30 Nov 20X6)
Net receivables in SOFP	$35,162	

415 C

416 $137,900

Cost of Sales = 100/130 × $182,000	$140,000
Less: reduction in inventory	($2,100)
Purchases	$137,900

417 $1,000

Credit purchases	$12,000
Less: paid	($1,000)
Payable at 30 June	$11,000

PARTNERSHIPS

418 C

The capital account of each partner does not record the share of profit each partner is allocated and nor does it reflect drawings. Those items are recorded in the current account of each partner. If a partner makes a loan to the partnership, it treated as a liability of the business, rather than additional capital introduced by that partner.

419 A

A salary paid to a partner is part of the appropriation of profit, and it not a business expense. Similarly, interest earned on capital accounts is part of the appropriation of profit between the partners and is recorded in the current account of each partner. Partners may have different capital account balances and will then usually be entitled to a different profit share.

420 B

There may be more than three persons in a partnership. Employees of a business cannot also be a partner in that business.

421 C

There is no legal requirement to have a partnership agreement; the Partnership Act will apply otherwise. It is normally an agreement confidential to the partners and set out many points on which the partners have agreed to carry on their business activities.

422 D

This would not be included within the partnership agreement, although items A, B and C would be included in the agreement.

423 C

	$	
Profit	27,800	
Less Salary – Bao	3,800	
Residual profit	24,000	
of which Viv's share is 3/5 or		$14,400

424 C

425 $4,800

Ali's share of the profit is calculated after deducting Dai's salary:
($16,000 – $8,000) × 3/5 = $4,800.

426 $24,250

	$	
Balance at 1 November 20X5	24,800	credit
Salary	6,500	credit
Interest on drawings	1,800	debit
Share of profit	12,750	credit
Drawings	18,000	debit
Balance at 31 October 20X6	24,250	credit

427 $430,000

$75,000 + $290,000 – $105,000 + $170,000 = $430,000

428 $52,750

($170,000 – (75,000 × 5%) – 8,000) = $158,250/3 = $52,750

429 $61,500

($15,000 × 5%) + 8,000 + $52,750 = $61,500

430 $9,548

Profit $30,709, less salary $14,000, thus available for appropriation = $16,709

Sam's share is 4/7 of this amount or $9,548.

431 A

	Total	**Kranti**	**Lazim**
	$	$	$
Profit for the year	73,540		
Salary to Kranti	(18,000)	18,000	
	55,540		
Profit share 2:3 × $59,540	(59,540)	22,216	33,324
		40,216	33,324

432 B

	Total	**Manvi**	**Nartan**
	$	$	$
Profit for the year	24,680		
Salary to Jane	(5,000)		5,000
	19,680		
Profit share 60:40 × $19,680	(19,680)	11,808	7,872
		11,808	12,872

433 $15,870

	Total	Pahal	Parul
	$	$	$
Profit for the year	52,900		
Salary to Paul and Linda	(20,000)	14,000	6,000
	32,900		
Profit share 7:3 × $32,900	(32,900)	23,030	9,870
		37,030	15,870

434 D

	Total	Pavi	Razz
	$	$	$
Profit for the year	36,600		
Salary to Razz	(12,500)		12,500
	24,100		
Profit share 90:10 × $24,100	(32,900)	21,690	2,410
		21,690	14,910

435 B

Current accounts		Reema	Rimple
	$	$	$
Balance b/f		21,735	14,876
Drawings		(27,500)	(26,500)
Profit for year	60,000		
Salary to Reema	(5,000)	5,000	
	55,000		
Profit share 3:5 × $55,000	(59,000)	20,625	34,375
		19,860	22,751

436 $19,860

See answer above for calculation.

437 $9,094

Current accounts		Kia	Ali
	$	$	$
Balance b/f		14,769	13,748
Drawings		(38,775)	(43,915)
Profit for year	80,000		
Salary to Kia and Ali	(6,000)	3,500	2,500
	74,000		
Profit share 2:3 × $75,000	(74,000)	29,600	44,400
		9,094	11,733

438 A

Owners' equity	
	$
Capital balances	50,000
Current balance b/f	20,625
Drawings	(34,500)
Profit for the year	150,000
	186,125

439 B

Residual profit share	
	$
Profit for the year	150,000
Interest on capital (5% × $50,000)	(2,500)
Sai – salary	(12,500)
Residual profit to share equally	135,000
Residual profit share per partner	45,000

440 C

Sai – total profit share	
	$
Interest on capital (5% × $20,000)	1,000
Sai – salary	12,500
Share of profit	45,000
	58,500

441 D

Sai – current account balance

	$
Balance b/f	7,000
Interest on capital (5% × $20,000)	1,000
Sai – salary	12,500
Share of profit	45,000
Drawings	(13,750)
	51,750

442 A

Total current account balance

	$
Total current account balances b/f	20,625
Total profit for the year	150,000
Total drawings for the year	(34,500)
	136,125

443 A

Residual profit share

	$
Profit for the year	45,000
Interest on capital (10% × $120,000)	(12,000)
Partnership salaries	(30,000)
Residual profit to share equally	3,000
Residual profit share per partner	1,000

Tutorial note

Note that interest on capital and partners' salaries are accounted for first as normal, and then any residual loss is dealt with in the profit sharing ratio between the partners.

444 D

	$
Interest on capital (10% × $50,000)	5,000
Partnership salary	8,000
Share of residual profit	1,000
	14,000

445

	Business expense	**Profit appropriation**
Salary paid to an employee	Correct	
Salary paid to a partner		Correct

'Salaries' paid to partners are an appropriation of profits, not an expense. Salary paid to an employee is a business expense.

446 A

Items B, C and D would normally be accounted for in the current account of each partner.

447 B

Accounting for goodwill on retirement of a partner is accounted for in the capital account.

448 D

$80,000 + $121,000 – $71,000 + $180,000 = $310,000

449 B

($180,000 – (80,000 × 4%) – 7,500) = $169,300 × 40% = $67,720

450 C

($28,000 × 4%) + 7,500 + ($169,300 × 40%) = $76,340

451

	Debit	**Credit**
Partners' capital accounts	Correct	
Goodwill		Correct

452 C

Goodwill is credited to the old partnership Nuwa and Suyin – $30,000 each. Goodwill is debited to the new partnership in the new profit-sharing ratio = $20,000 to each partner. This gives a debit balance of $20,000 on Maz's capital account. To clear this and have a credit balance of $10,000, Maz must contribute $30,000 upon joining the partnership.

453 B

Ali retirement – total amount due

	$
Capital balance b/f	60,000
Current balance b/f	15,000
Share of goodwill (1/3 × $60,000)	20,000
	95,000

454 C

Goodwill is credited to the old partnership in the profit-sharing ratio 4:2. This will amount to $50,000 to Jo and $25,000 to Terri. Goodwill is debited to the new partnership in the new profit-sharing ratio: $25,000 for each partner. This gives a debit balance of $25,000 on Maz's capital account. To clear this and have a credit balance of $5,000, Maz must contribute $30,000 upon joining the partnership.

455

Vic retirement – total amount due

	$
Capital balance b/f	25,000
Current balance b/f	5,000
Share of goodwill (1/3 × $90,000)	30,000
	60,000

Section 5

SPECIMEN EXAM QUESTIONS

Section A – ALL 50 questions are compulsory and MUST be attempted

Each question is worth 2 marks.

1 Sybil's Which of the following accounting principles is most relevant in relation to the requirements of IAS *16 Property, Plant and Equipment* in the following situations financial year ended on 30 November 20X2. She incurred the same telephone expense each month. The last invoice paid for telephone calls was $1,800. This invoice covered the three months to 31 October 20X2.

What adjustment is required in respect of telephone expenses when preparing the accounts to 30 November 20X2?

A An accrual of $1,200

B A prepayment of $1,200

C A prepayment of $600

D An accrual of $600

2 **Which of the following accounting principles is most relevant in relation to the requirements of IAS 16 *Property, Plant and Equipment* in the following situations?**

	Accruals	Going concern
Depreciating property, plant and equipment		
Classifying property as a non-current asset		

3 Norman is entering information into the non-current asset register.

Which TWO of the following pieces of information will be used when carrying out a verification of the physical presence of non-current assets?

	Selected answer
Supplier	
Location	
Description	
Cost	

4 John has been asked to provide a copy of his final accounts to his bank manager

What is the bank manager MOST likely to use the final accounts for?

A To calculate the tax payable on John's business profit

B To ensure that the profit is sufficient to provide a good income for John

C To ensure that the business is able to make the repayments on a loan

D To ensure that John's profit margin is as good as the margin earned by other bank customers

5 In preparing the financial statements, it was discovered that an asset purchased for $10,000 in the last month of the accounting period had been debited to repairs in error. Depreciation is charged at 15% per annum on a monthly pro-rata basis.

Are the following statements relating to the correction of the error true or false?

	True	**False**
The error would need to be corrected before the financial statements were finalised		
The correction will decrease the profit for the year		

6 **Which of the following statements correctly describes the dual aspect convention of accounting?**

A A change in the value of assets leads to an equal change in the value of liabilities plus capital

B Only two ledger accounts will be needed to record any transaction

C If a transaction requires two debit entries, two credit entries must also be made

D Transactions are recorded in both the general ledger and in a separate detailed listing

7 Janet valued her inventory at 30 June 20X5 at its cost of $22,960. This includes some items which cost $1,950 which have been difficult to sell. Janet intends to have these items repacked at a cost of $400. She can then sell them for $900.

What will be the value of closing inventory in Janet's accounts at 30 June 20X5?

$

8 A business has cash of $1,100, trade payables of $2,500, a mortgage liability of $8,000 and land of $16,000.

What is the capital balance?

A $10,500

B $20,400

C $6,600

D $16,000

9 Adele runs a restaurant. In August 20X3 she received a letter from a lawyer representing a customer who claims he suffered food poisoning after eating in the restaurant. The customer is claiming damages of $3,000. Adele offered to pay $300. Her lawyer's advice is that in the event of the case going to court, she is likely to be required to pay $1,500. The solicitor also advised that the court case is unlikely to take place before April 20X4.

What amount should be provided for in respect of the claim in Adele's final accounts for the year ended 30 September 20X3?

A $1,500

B $nil

C $300

D $3,000

10 Ruth started trading a year ago. She sells her products at a mark-up of 30%. In the first year of trading, she bought goods for $25,800. Her sales in the year were $30,888.

What is the value of Ruth's closing inventory?

$

11 Fiona received a statement of account from a supplier, Raj, showing a balance outstanding to Raj of $15,400 at 31 December 20X8. Fiona's accounting system shows a balance outstanding to Raj of $16,200 at 31 December 20X8.

From Fiona's accounting perspective, which TWO of the following statements could explain the difference?

	Selected answer
Raj had given Fiona a credit note for goods returned which had been omitted from Raj's supplier account in Fiona's accounting system	
Fiona had made a payment to Raj before the year end which had not been reflected on the statement of account	
Fiona had a recorded a purchase invoice from Raj in Raj's supplier account in Fiona's accounting system twice	
Fiona had recorded a payment to a different supplier and allocated it incorrectly to Raj's account in Fiona's accounting system	

12 Ari is registered to account for sales tax and he has purchased goods for resale. The invoice shows the cost of the goods as $357.50, which includes sales tax at 10%.

What debit entry should be made in the purchases account?

A $357.50

B $393.25

C $325.00

D $321.75

13 At 1 September 20X1 the balance on Hai's capital account was $31,754. In the year to 31 August 20X2 he invested an additional amount of $40,000 of personal funds and took a loan of $80,000 for the business. The statement of profit or loss for the year to 31 August 20X2 reported a profit of $48,634 and Hai's drawings during the year were $28,500.

What is Hal's closing capital at 31 August 20X2?

$

14 When Frank prepared his year end accounts, he made a calculation error and overstated the value of his closing inventory.

What is the effect of this error on the profit for the year and the net assets at the year end?

	Understated	**Overstated**
Profit for the year		
Net assets at year end		

15 John needs to adjust his draft year-end accounts to record a prepayment if $1,500 and an accrual of $400,

How will John's profit and net assets be affected by including the prepayment and the accrual?

A	Profit will increase by $1,100	Net assets will reduce by $1,100
B	Profit will reduce by $1,900	Net assets will increase by $1,900
C	Profit will increase by $1,100	Net assets will increase by $1,100
D	Profit will reduce by $1,900	Net assets will reduce by $1,900

16 One of Brian's customers returned goods valued at $670. These had been sold on credit.

What double entry should Brian post to record the return of the goods?

A	Dr Trade receivables $670	Cr Bank $670
B	Dr Bank $670	Cr Trade receivables $670
C	Dr Trade receivables $670	Cr Sales returns $670
D	Dr Sales returns $670	Cr Trade receivables $670

17 Michael and Donald have been in partnership for several years, sharing profits and losses in the ratio 3:4. At 1 January 20X4 the business had the following credit balances on the partners' capital and current accounts:

	Capital	**Current**
	$	$
Michael	65,000	11,486
Donald	80,000	9,637

The partnership statement of profit or loss for the year to 31 December 20X4 disclosed a net profit of $28,595, and the partners made drawings of $16,500 each.

What is the balance brought down on Michael's current account at 31 December?

$

18 At 1 October 20X1, Bakari's bank overdraft was $3,270. During the year to 30 September 20X2, he made electronic bank transfers with a total value of $189,642. His total lodgements during the year were $191,729. In addition, bank charges of $827 were incurred.

What is Bakari's bank balance carried forward at 30 September 20X2 as per his accounting records?

A $2,010 credit

B $356 credit

C $4,530 debit

D $6,184 debit

19 **Which of the following items would be included in the statement of financial position and which in the statement of profit or loss?**

	Statement of financial position	**Statement of profit or loss**
Cost of sales		
Provisions		
Depreciation expense		
Capital		

20 Desmond is registered for sales tax. The tax rate is 17.5%. The following transactions occurred during the quarter ended 31 March 20X3:

	Sales including sales tax	Purchases including sales tax
	$	$
January	5,875	3,525
February	8,225	4,700
March	7,050	5,875

What is the balance on the sales tax account at 31 March 20X3?

A $1,223.75 due from the tax authority

B $1,050 due to the tax authority

C $1,223.75 due to the tax authority

D $1,050 due from the tax authority

21 Riley has been trading as a retailer of shoes for many years. During the current year, Riley required more funds to expand his business so paid $20,000 into his business bank account from his personal savings.

Which TWO of the following would be the dual effect of the above transaction for Riley's business?

	Selected answer
Increase in capital	
Decrease in capital	
Increase in assets	
Decrease in assets	

22 At 1 January 20X3 Wasan had 250 units of inventory. These were valued at $155 each. During January, the purchases and sales of the item were:

Date	Purchases	Sales
5 January		175 units
10 January	140 units at $158 per unit	
17 January		130 units
22 January	110 units at $160 per unit	
28 January		105 units

Wasan values inventory on the periodic weighted average basis.

What is the value of Wasan's inventory at 31 January 20X3 (to the nearest $1)?

A $14,400

B $14,190

C $14,125

D $14,299

23 Margaret compared her bank statement with the bank account in her general ledger and found the balances did not agree. She found two possible causes for the difference.

Do these reasons for the difference require an entry in the bank general ledger account?

	Yes	No
Some cheques have not been lodged by her suppliers		
The bank debited fees on her account		

24 Alex and Jose are in partnership. Under the terms of the partnership, Alex is entitled to a salary of $11,000 per annum. In the year to 31 December 20X1, the net profit of the partnership was $43,877. Interest on capital and interest on drawings for the year have been calculated as:

	Alex	**Jose**
Interest on capital	$8,000	$9,500
Interest on drawings	$3,500	$5,400

What was the residual profit for the year ended 31 December 20X1?

$

25 **Which of the following statements regarding inventory valuation is correct?**

A Inventory should be valued at anticipated selling price less any cost which will be incurred

B All items held in inventory should be valued at cost

C Inventory valuation should exclude profit which has not yet been earned

D The purchase price of items which have been held for the longest period is an acceptable method for valuing inventory

26 **What is the purpose of charging depreciation?**

A To allocate the cost of a non-current asset over the accounting periods expected to benefit from its use

B To ensure that funds are available for the eventual replacement of the non-current asset

C To reflect the fair value of an asset in the statement of financial position

D To reflect the falling realisable value of an asset

27 Samantha has prepared the following bank reconciliation statement at 31 March:

	$
Balance on bank statement	1,250 (overdrawn)
Unpresented cheques	748
Outstanding lodgement	2,200
Balance on ledger account	202 (debit)

How should the bank balance be reported in Samantha's statement of financial position as at 31 March?

A $1,250 as a current liability

B $1,250 as a current asset

C $202 as a current liability

D $202 as a current asset

28 At the start of the year, the balance on Toni's capital account was $35,869. During the year Toni made drawings of $17,800 and the net profit for the year was $18,700.

What is Toni's closing capital at the end of the year?

$

29 At 30 November, Charles is owed a total of $72,660 by his customers. His receivables allowance brought forward from the previous year end was $11,700. He estimated that his receivables allowance should be equivalent to 15% of the amounts due from customers.

What amount should be included in the statement of profit or loss for the irrecoverable debts expense for the year to 30 November?

A $801 debit

B $10,899 debit

C $801 credit

D $10,899 credit

30 Sarah's bank general ledger account at 30 April 20X4 shows a debit balance of $2,280. Comparison with the bank statement at the same date reveals the following differences:

	$
Uncleared electronic payments	780
Bank charges not in the bank general ledger account	40
Receipts not yet credited by the bank	450
Dishonoured cheque not in the bank general ledger	120

What is the reconciled bank general ledger account balance at 30 April 20X4?

A $1,340

B $1,950

C $2,120

D $2,360

31 Maura and Carrie have been in partnership sharing profits and losses equally. At 1 March 20X1 the total value of their capital and current balances was $225,000. At that date Delia was admitted to the partnership and it was agreed that:

1 The partners would share profits and losses equally

2 Goodwill in the business would be valued at $75,000

3 Goodwill would not be maintained in the books of the partnership

4 Delia would introduce cash to ensure that her opening capital balance is nil

How much cash must Delia contribute?

A $75,000

B $25,000

C $37,500

D $12,500

32 **How should prompt payment discounts be treated where a customer unexpectedly takes advantage of the discount?**

A As an expense included in cost of sales

B As a deduction from the value of sales

C As a deduction from the value of discount received

D As an expense deducted from gross profit

33 Jessie's trial balance at 30 September 20X0 included:

	Debit	**Credit**
	$	$
Trade receivables ledger	90,350	
Allowance for irrecoverable debts brought forward		2,490

The following information is also available:

1 No entries have been made in respect of cash of $1,320 received from Jeffrey whose balance had been written off in the previous accounting year, and

2 At 30 September 20X0 an irrecoverable balance of $1,950 is to be written off and the receivable allowance is to be adjusted to 1.5% of the remaining balance

What figure will be reported in the statement of financial position at 30 September for trade receivables?

$ ____

34 In finalising the financial statements for the year ended 30 September 20X9, it was discovered that an invoice of $1,380 which was received on 12 November 20X9 in respect of insurance for the six months ended 31 October 20X9 had not been accounted for.

Which of the following journal entries are required to account for the invoice received?

A	Dr Insurance expenses $1,380	Cr Accruals $1,380 800
B	Dr Insurance expenses $1,150	Cr Accruals $1,150
C	Dr Prepayments $230	Cr Insurance expenses $230
D	Dr Prepayments $1,380	Cr Insurance expenses $1,380

35 Alan purchased a machine on 1 March 20X1 for $12,000. He incurred additional costs for transportation of $1,300 and installation of $2,000. Shortly after he started to use the machine, it broke down and the repairs of the machine cost $600. Alan charges depreciation at 10% per annum on a straight line basis with a full year's charge in the year of acquisition.

What was the correct carrying amount of the machine at 31 December 20X1?

A $10,800

B $13,770

C $14,370

D $15,300

36 Luis and David are in partnership sharing profits and losses in the ratio 3:2. David is entitled to a salary of $9,000 and interest on capital is paid at a rate of 8% per annum. The partners' capital balances are:

Luis	$75,000
David	$60,000

The partnership statement of profit or loss for the year shows a profit of $58,500.

How much of the total profit is Luis entitled to?

$

37 Which of the following correctly states the accounting equation?

A Assets plus capital equals liabilities

B Capital plus liabilities equals assets

C Assets plus liabilities equals capital

D Capital minus liabilities equals assets

38 Fred purchased a new van. The new van cost $9,000 and Fred paid a cheque for $2,500 to the dealer. In addition the dealer accepted an old van in part exchange. The old van had been bought three years ago for $11,600 and had been depreciated by $6,750.

What is the gain or loss or loss on disposal of the old van?

A $1,650 profit

B $6,500 profit

C $1,650 loss

D $6,500 loss

39 Lance is registered for sales tax and is entering a purchase invoice into the accounting system. The invoice shows the following costs:

	$
Water treatment equipment	39,800
Delivery	1,100
Maintenance charge	3,980
Sales tax	7,854
Invoice total	52,734

What is the total value of asset expenditure on the invoice?

A $52,734

B $44,880

C $39,800

D $40,900

40 The computerised accounting system has produced a report showing a summary of year-end manual adjustments which have been made, extracts of which are shown below:

	Trial balance		**Adjustments**	
	Dr	**Cr**	**Dr**	**Cr**
	$	$	$	$
Rent and rates	18,000		3,000	
Stationery	3,000			1,200

Which TWO of the following statements are correct?

	Selected answer
Rent and rates will be shown in the statement of profit or loss as an expense of $21,000	
Rent and rates will be shown in the statement of profit or loss as an expense of $15,000	
Stationery will be shown in the statement of profit or loss as an expense of $4,200	
Stationery will be shown in the statement of profit or loss as an expense of $1,800	

41 Nandita bought goods for resale on credit from Pascale. The goods cost $600 before sales tax, which is calculated at 10%.

When the transaction is posted to the general ledger, which TWO of the following entries should be included?

	Selected answer
Cr Trade payables	
Dr Purchases	
Cr Sales tax	
Cr Bank	

42 At 30 September 20X3 Pamela's inventory was valued at $6,400 and her trial balance included the following balances:

	Debit	Credit
	$	$
Sales		45,000
Purchases	29,500	
Inventory at 1 October 20X2	5,700	
Carriage inwards	750	
Postage	340	
Wages	6,000	
Advertising	1,900	
Other expenses	2,500	

What was Pamela's gross profit for the year ended 30 September 20X3?

A $4,710

B $15,110

C $15,450

D $16,200

43 **Which of the following best describes a statement of profit or loss?**

A It is a statement that presents all the ledger account balances

B It is a statement that shows the cash inflows or outflows of a business for an accounting period

C It is a statement that shows the financial performance of a business for an accounting period

D It is a statement that shows a business's financial position at a point in time

44 Consider the following statements about going concern:

1 Financial statements must always be prepared on the going concern basis

2 If a business is not considered to be a going concern, financial statements should not be prepared.

Which of the statements is/are correct?

A 2 only

B 1 only

C Both 1 and 2

D Neither 1 nor 2

45 At 30 November 20X3, Zoltan's bank current account was overdrawn. He also had a bank loan on which monthly capital repayments of the principal will commence in February 20X5.

How should these balances be reported on his statement of financial position at 30 November 20X3?

	Current asset	**Current liability**	**Non-current liability**
Bank Loan			
Bank current account			

46 James has been advised that one of his customers has ceased trading and that he will not recover the balance of $720 owed by his customer.

What entry should James make in his general ledger?

A Dr Trade receivables $720 Cr Irrecoverable debts $720

B Dr Irrecoverable debts $720 Cr Trade receivables $720

C Dr Trade receivables $720 Cr Bank $720

D Dr Bank $720 Cr Trade receivables $720

47 **Identify whether the following costs should be included in the cost of inventories in accordance with IAS 2 *Inventories*?**

	Should be included	**Should not be included**
Transport costs of imported raw materials		
Storage costs of finished goods		
General administrative overheads		
Selling costs		

48 The amount owed to Jane by her customers at 31 October 20X2 was \$34,729. A year earlier she was owed \$27,641. During the year Jane had deposited \$327,684 to her bank account. This included payments received from her credit customers as well as \$45,000 which Jane had received from the sale of her holiday home.

What was the value of Jane's sales for the year ended 31 October 20X2?

A \$289,772

B \$334,772

C \$327,684

D \$282,684

49 Juan and Bilal are in partnership sharing profits in the ratio 2:3 respectively. The partnership statement of profit or loss reported a net profit for the year of \$115,000. Juan is to receive a salary of \$10,000 per annum.

What is Juan's total share of the profit of \$115,000?

\$

50 **Which accounting principle is applied when two similar transactions are treated in the same way?**

A Materiality

B Consistency

C Accruals

D Duality

(Total: 100 marks)

Section 6

ANSWERS TO SPECIMEN EXAM QUESTIONS

1 D

November 20X2 telephone payment is accrued.

Payment for November 20X2 = \$1,800 ÷ 3 = \$600

2 A

3

	Selected answer
Supplier	
Location	Correct
Description	Correct
Cost	

4 C

5

	True	**False**
The error would need to be corrected before the financial statements were finalised	Correct	
The correction will decrease the profit for the year		Correct

6 A

7 \$21,510

\$22,960 – \$1,950 + (\$900 – \$400) = \$22,510

8 C

\$16,000 + \$1,100 – \$2,500 – \$8,000 = \$6,600

9 A

10 $2,040

$25,800 – ($30,888/1.3) = $2,040

11

	Selected answer
Raj had given Fiona a credit note for goods returned which had been omitted from Raj's supplier account in Fiona's accounting system	Correct
Fiona had made a payment to Raj before the year end which had not been reflected on the statement of account	
Fiona had a recorded a purchase invoice from Raj in Raj's supplier account in Fiona's accounting system twice	
Fiona had recorded a payment to a different supplier and allocated it incorrectly to Raj's account in Fiona's accounting system	Correct

12 C

$357.50/ (1 + 0.10) = $325.00

13 $91,888

Bal b/f $31,754 + Cap Intro $40,000 + Profit $48,634 – Drawings $28,500 = $91,888

14

	Understated	**Overstated**
Profit for the year		Correct
Net assets at year end		Correct

15 C

16 D

17 $7,241 Credit

Bal b/f $11,486 + Profit share $12,255 – Drawings $16,500 = $7,241 credit

18 A

Bank o/d b/f ($3,270) – chqs issued $189,642 + lodgements $191,729 – bank charges $827 = $2,010 overdrawn i.e. credit balance

19

	Statement of financial position	**Statement of profit or loss**
Cost of sales		Correct
Provisions	Correct	
Depreciation expense		Correct
Capital	Correct	

20 B

21

	Selected answer
Increase in capital	Correct
Decrease in capital	
Increase in assets	Correct
Decrease in assets	

22 C

Periodic weighted average rate:

[(250 × \$155) + (140 × \$158) + (110 × \$160)]/(250 + 140 + 110) = \$156.94

Closing inventory (units) = 250 – 175 + 140 – 130 + 110 – 105 = 90

Closing inventory (value) = \$156.94 × 90 = \$14,125

23

	Yes	**No**
Some cheques have not been lodged by her suppliers		No
The bank debited fees on her account	Yes	

24 \$24,277

Net profit \$43,877 – Salary \$11,000 – Int on capital \$17,500 + Int on drawings \$8,900 = \$24,277.

25 C

26 A

27 D

28 $36,769

Balance b/f $35,869 – drawings $17,800 + profit $18,700 = $36,769

29 C

$11,700 – (15% of $72,660) = $801 credit

30 C

$2,280 – $40 – $120 = $2,120

31 B

Delia would need to introduce capital of contribute capital 1/3 of $75,000 = $25,000. Remember that goodwill is credited to the goodwill account (to remove it from the accounting records) and the ''new partners' are debited in their profit-sharing ratio i.e. $25,000 is credited to the capital account of each partner. Delia must therefore introduce capital of $25,000.

32 B

33 $87,074

$90,350 – $1,950 – 1.5% of ($90,350 – $1,950) = $87,074

34 B

35 B

$12,000 + $1,300 + $2,000 – 10% of ($12,000 + $1,300 + $2,000) = $13,770

36 $29,220

Available profit $58,500 – $9,000 – 8% of 75,000 – 8% of 60,000) = $38,700
Luis share (3/5) × $38,700 + Interest on capital = $23,220 + $6,000 = $29,220

37 B

38 A

$9,000 – ($2,500 + ($11,600 – $6,750)) = $1,650 gain

39 D

$39,800 + $1,100 = $40,900. Note that sales tax is not part of the cost recognized as an asset.

40

	Selected answer
Rent and rates will be shown in the statement of profit or loss as an expense of $21,000	Correct
Rent and rates will be shown in the statement of profit or loss as an expense of $15,000	
Stationery will be shown in the statement of profit or loss as an expense of $4,200	
Stationery will be shown in the statement of profit or loss as an expense of $1,800	Correct

41

	Selected answer
Cr Trade payables	Correct
Dr Purchases	Correct
Cr Sales tax	
Cr Bank	

42 C

$45,000 + $6,400 – ($29,500 + $5,700 + $750) = $15,450

43 C

44 D

45

	Current asset	**Current liability**	**Non-current liability**
Bank Loan			Correct
Bank current account		Correct	

46 B

47

	Should be included	**Should not be included**
Transport costs of imported raw materials	Correct	
Storage costs of finished goods		Correct
General administrative overheads		Correct
Selling costs		Correct

48 A

$327,684 – $45,000 + ($34,729 – $27,641) = $289,772

49 $44,000

50 B

Section 7

REFERENCES

The Board (2025) *Conceptual Framework for Financial Reporting*. London: IFRS Foundation.

The Board (2025) *IAS 2 Inventories*. London: IFRS Foundation.

The Board (2025) *IAS 16 Property, Plant and Equipment*. London: IFRS Foundation.

The Board (2025) *IAS 37 Provisions, Contingent Liabilities and Contingent Assets*. London: IFRS Foundation.

The Board (2025) *IFRS 15 Revenue from Contracts with Customers*. London: IFRS Foundation.

The Board (2025) *IFRS 18 Presentation and Disclosure in Financial Statements*